Learning About Psychology

Second Edition

Bruce B. Svare, PhD

 CENGAGE
Learning·

Australia • Brazil • Japan • Korea • Mexico • Singapore • Spain • United Kingdom • United States

Learning About Psychology: Second Edition

Learning About Psychology, Second Edition
Bruce B. Svare, PhD

© 2009 Cengage Learning. All rights reserved.

Executive Editors:
Maureen Staudt
Michael Stranz

Senior Project Development Manager:
Linda deStefano

Marketing Specialist:
Courtney Sheldon

Senior Production/Manufacturing Manager:
Donna M. Brown

Production Editorial Manager:
Kim Fry

Sr. Rights Acquisition Account Manager:
Todd Osborne

For product information and technology assistance, contact us at
Cengage Learning Customer & Sales Support, 1-800-354-9706
For permission to use material from this text or product,
submit all requests online at **cengage.com/permissions**
Further permissions questions can be emailed to
permissionrequest@cengage.com

This book contains select works from existing Cengage Learning resources and was produced by Cengage Learning Custom Solutions for collegiate use. As such, those adopting and/or contributing to this work are responsible for editorial content accuracy, continuity and completeness.

Compilation © 2012 Cengage Learning
ISBN-13: 978-1-285-00799-1

ISBN-10: 1-285-00799-9

Cengage Learning
5191 Natorp Boulevard
Mason, Ohio 45040
USA
Cengage Learning is a leading provider of customized learning solutions with office locations around the globe, including Singapore, the United Kingdom, Australia, Mexico, Brazil, and Japan. Locate your local office at:
international.cengage.com/region.

Cengage Learning products are represented in Canada by Nelson Education, Ltd.
For your lifelong learning solutions, visit **www.cengage.com/custom.**
Visit our corporate website at **www.cengage.com.**

Printed in the United States of America

CONTENTS

PART III   KEY SLIDES

PART IV   PRACTICE EXAMS AND ANSWERS

Part I. Achieving Success in Psychology 101

THE GOAL OF THIS BOOK

How can I do better in Psychology 101 at SUNY-Albany? Every year I hear this question pronounced many times from freshman who are seeking ways to improve upon their academic performance. For some, it is too late while for others it is just in time. Regardless, there are things that new students of Psychology 101 can do to position themselves for success in this class.

Just what does it take to achieve academic success? Simply put, it takes an open mind, a willingness to make a commitment to change, and a desire to be engaged in the learning experience. It can be done, but oftentimes it is not easy to change habits that were learned long ago and are now counterproductive. Clearly, every student has a choice and the ultimate decision on change is the student's and the student's alone. It is my hope that every one of you will benefit in some way from the information presented here, and that it will have a positive impact upon your enjoyment and performance in this class.

The information compiled in this book, *Learning About Psychology*, represents my accumulated experiences teaching a subject that I have loved....the study of behavior. I have talked with thousands of introductory psychology students through the years about their successes and failures. I have learned what works and what doesn't work. The information they have provided, as well as my own thoughts and opinions, have shaped my ideas on how students can perform well in this class.

I have taught introductory psychology for over 30 years to thousands of college students. Each semester I teach this class, I typically give about 10% As, 20% Bs, 40% Cs, 20% Ds, and 10% Es. Although there are fluctuations in this "normal" distribution from semester to semester, this pattern has not substantially changed through the years.

Can performance change in this class and can students do better than they have in the past? I would not have written this book if I did not feel that this was the case. Indeed, it would please me no end if everyone took the information here and applied it to their own particular circumstance. Maybe this class will be the first to receive all As during my stay here at SUNY-Albany!

Have students changed substantially since I have been at SUNY-Albany? In some ways yes and in other ways no. With each passing year, I am amazed at the increasing sophistication of many incoming students as they take the journey through my classes. Studious, well-prepared, and exceptionally organized, they invariably do what it takes to succeed in my class as well as their other courses. At the same time, I am also concerned with how ill-prepared many students are each year. They can not cope with the demands of my introductory psychology class and college course work in general. As a result, they do average or below average work and never fulfill their potential.

SUNY-Albany admissions standards are amongst the most stringent in the State University system and our students have performed well in their high school classes and SAT exams. In spite of their stellar academic records and in spite of their potential to do better, many new students each semester end up performing poorly or only do average work.

Why do some students perform poorly, others do average work, and still others experience great success in this class? I am not sure that I necessarily have the answer to that question. My experience through the years suggests that the reasons for poor performance are probably multi-determined and there is not one single causal factor. More importantly, however, I do know that everyone has the capability of performing very well in this class as well as their other classes if they are willing to pay attention to a few simple keys for academic success. Thus, *Learning About Psychology* was motivated by my desire to give new students of psychology a "jump start" and a friendly guide to success in Psychology 101. While written for my Psychology 101 students, many of the suggestions here can easily be applied to other classes as well.

Will reading this book and following some of its suggestions necessarily *guarantee* a good grade in this class? It most certainly *will not* and I want to provide that disclaimer right from the start. There is no substitute for hard work and there are no shortcuts to academic success. This book will set you on the right path, position you to perform better, and assist you in making decisions about how you should distribute your valuable time. After that, it is really up to you and your own personal desire to succeed and do well. Make no mistake about it, this book is not a magic pill or a cure all for low motivation, poor habits, and a lackadaisical attitude toward college. No amount of "inside information" and experience can possibly overcome those fatal flaws that serve to undermine academic success.

THE RECIPE FOR SUCCESS

What are the keys to success in this class? I have identified 7 ingredients that are instrumental for outstanding achievement in Psychology 101. In no particular order of importance, they are listed here:

- The "art" of understanding psychology
- Understanding and executing the class requirements
- Coming to class prepared and taking good notes
- Preparing for and taking examinations and quizzes
- Completing the research participation requirement efficiently
- Closely monitoring your own performance
- Getting help when you need it

I have compared all of this to a recipe that one would use in cooking. If the ingredients are all added together in the proper amounts, then the outcome will be successful. If any one ingredient is missing and/or the proper amounts of any one ingredient are not used, then the end product could be disastrous. Let us examine each one of these essential components and what they mean to achieving success in Introductory Psychology.

THE ART OF UNDERSTANDING PSYCHOLOGY

Believe it or not, there is an art to understanding the discipline of psychology. Once learned, it can make everything easier for you. I can explain this art best by offering up an analogy to sports.

Let's say that you wanted to become a good basketball player. First, you would make it a point to learn the rules and theory of the game. Second, you would have to learn the fundamentals of the game such as dribbling the ball, passing, shooting, rebounding the ball, and playing defense. Third, you would have to combine the rules and fundamentals of the game to constant practice in combination with learning the team nature of the sport. Finally, you would have to test or apply what you have learned by participating in actual competitive situations against other teams.

Learning psychology is no different than learning the game of basketball. One must first learn the language and theory of psychology. Second, you must learn the methods of psychology to enable you to interpret the latest research. Third, you must constantly practice what you have learned so that you can truly master the topic. Fourth, you must demonstrate competence in the discipline of psychology by applying what you have learned to real life situations and executing this competence in a test situation.

Every profession and every discipline has its own specific language and theory. Psychology is no different. There are words that are unique to psychology and theoretical underpinnings that guide those words and their meanings. With each new topic that is addressed, we will spend considerable time understanding the underlying theory and the language that is unique to its meaning.

Psychology also has its own methodology. It uses the scientific method just as all the sciences do, but it also uses procedures that are unique to the discipline. Learning about these procedures is instrumental to understanding the discipline of psychology. We will spend considerable time during this class learning about the methods and procedures psychologists use to collect behavioral information.

Practicing what you have learned is important for success in any field and psychology is no different. As you are learning the methods, theories, and concepts of psychology, you must have ways of exploring your competence and filling in the gaps. This is done through self-testing practice exams and quizzes.

Finally, you must be able to demonstrate mastery of the subject matter of psychology. It is my aim to get you to think like a psychologist by applying what you have learned to real life. This is done by assessing your mastery of the material by way of standardized tests and quizzes in which there is a heavy emphasis upon applying theory, language, and concepts to real life problems and situations.

Does all of this sound quite simple to you? It should because none of it is really that novel. What you have read so far should not shock you or surprise you. But, you need to be constantly reminded of the art of understanding psychology since it is instrumental to your success. Now, let's focus on the actual nuts and bolts of achieving success in this class.

UNDERSTANDING THE CLASS REQUIREMENTS

Early in the semester, you will be given two very important pieces of written information. You will receive the syllabus for the course as well as a handout describing the research participation requirement. Very little class time will be spent describing each. Therefore, it is imperative that you read this information several times thoroughly and carefully. READING THIS INFORMATION A NUMBER OF TIMES AND UNDERSTANDING ITS CONTENTS IS CRITICAL TO YOUR SUCCESS IN THIS CLASS. IT CAN MEAN THE DIFFERENCE BETWEEN ACHIEVING SUCCESS IN PSYCHOLOGY 101 OR PERFORMING POORLY!

It is distressing to me how frequently I have students who do not read the handouts and are totally unaware of the requirements for the class. Invariably they miss lectures, quizzes, and exams and generally end up with failing grades in the class. Ignorance of important requirements is no excuse in Psychology 101 or any other college course.

The syllabus covers the essentials like texts, office hours, grading policies for quizzes and exams, reading and exam schedule, and the consequences for academic dishonesty.

The handout regarding the research participation requirement is equally important. It goes over in painstaking detail how you are to complete this essential class requirement. Roughly 20% of the class will receive an incomplete in the course because they did not read this handout carefully.

If you have questions regarding the course requirements you should never hesitate to ask. Chances are someone else in the class also needs help with the same question. However, I often field unnecessary questions from students that usually result from a less than thorough reading of the handouts. Don't waste your time, the time of your classmates, and my time because you did not carefully read the material in the handouts.

Does all of this seem easy? It is easy! All you have to do is read a few sheets of paper that clearly spell everything out. But sadly, a significant number of you will not achieve success in this class simply because you did not bother to read the syllabus or the research participation requirement. Cut yourself a break and read both carefully. I guarantee you that it will save some heartache down the road.

COMING TO CLASS PREPARED AND TAKING GOOD NOTES

Coming to class on time, being prepared to listen and absorb information, and taking good notes in class are all essential parts of achieving success in this class. While this may sound silly and unnecessary to say for college students with a significant monetary investment in their academic careers, you would be amazed at how frequently students do not fulfill their end of the learning arrangement. Every semester, I have students who do not keep up with assigned reading material, always come late to class (or do not come to class at all!) and then proceed to sleep at their desk, and rarely take notes in class. This is a recipe for disaster and invariably these students end up doing very poorly in class.

Attending class is something that is purely up to you. You will note that professors at SUNY-Albany rarely if ever take roll. Thus, with the new found freedom that you have, it will be easy to cut class and go unnoticed. This is especially true in large survey courses held in the lecture center where you will be one of 300 or 400 other students in your class. Thus, you have the option of attending class or not. It is your choice and no one will be deducting points from you if you decide not to come. Importantly, however, what goes on in class is instrumental to your understanding the subject matter of psychology. You will not perform well on the exams and quizzes if you do not attend class. I have never had a student achieve success in this class if they did not attend class and fully engage themselves in the learning experience.

Just attending class however is not enough. You must come to class prepared. You will see on the syllabus that there is reading required of you for each lecture. It is very important that you complete the reading in your texts prior to a particular lecture. If you come into class cold without having read background material, the chances are high that you will soon be frustrated. You will be lost in a sea of information that you do not understand and you will be hopelessly behind 10 minutes into the lecture. Keeping up with your reading in preparation for the lectures is an essential part of doing well in the class.

Your ability to take good notes is also high on the list of essential skills in this class. Having success on exams and quizzes is contingent upon your diligence in classroom note-taking. Contained in this book is a complete lecture outline for Psychology 101 which you should bring with you to each class. It is set up in such a manner that all you have to do is follow my lectures and fill in the content under each heading and subheading. This should make some of the work involved in note-taking much easier since you can focus your attention on content rather than organizational structure.

A key aspect of note-taking is reviewing your notes immediately after class. If there are gaps in your notes and/or there are things that you don't understand, it is much easier to rectify these situations right away in contrast to a few days before an exam when catching up is almost impossible. If you should miss a class, it is of course permissible to borrow notes from a classmate. Certainly, you should come and see me during my office hours if there is material you do not understand.

This book also contains selected key powerpoint slides that are used during my lectures. You can refer to these slides as we cover material in the course. Keep in mind that these slides are not a substitute for reading the text assignments before coming to class and taking good notes while attending lectures. Just reading the slides and not coming to class is a recipe for disaster. My lectures are meant to enhance what is found in the powerpoint slides and to assist students in understanding important material.

Finally, at the beginning of every semester, I have urged students in the past to secure what I call a "study-buddy." This is someone you know in class who you can depend on for notes should you not be able to attend. It is also a person who you can study with periodically in case there is material that you do not fully comprehend. Of course, coming to see me during my office hours is also a good strategy when there is material you do not understand. However, please don't expect me to give a personalized lecture to you for a class you have missed. I am happy to discuss gaps you may have in your understanding of material but I won't repeat a lecture simply because you were not present for a particular class.

PREPARING FOR AND TAKING EXAMINATIONS AND QUIZZES

"What material am I responsible for on each exam?" Every semester I hear this question repeated by many students. This is a reasonable question to ask and my answer for the last 30 years has always been the same. You are responsible for all of the material presented in class as well as all of the material presented in the books you have been assigned to read. Please note very carefully, you are responsible for all of the material in the books regardless of whether it was presented in class or not.

Obviously, you would be wise to pay a bit more attention to the material presented in lecture that is also emphasized in the books you have read. Chances are relatively high that there will be a fair number of questions that will come from the material that has been emphasized in both places. However, you should not exclude from your studying material that is only presented in the books or material that is only presented in lecture. I have always believed that a good test should separate those that work very hard versus those that only do enough to get bye.

Therefore, there will always be a fair number of questions on each exam taken from material that we did not necessarily spend much time on or did not review at all.

There are four things you can do to enhance your chances of doing well on the exams. First, attend class religiously and take good notes. Second, regularly study your notes and your texts each day. It is preferable to review your lecture notes, key slides and text each day. Don't commit the cardinal sin of waiting until just a few nights before an exam to start your studying. This will only spell disaster since you will never be able to consolidate so much material in such a short span of time. Third, use the practice exams and quizzes that are included in this book. These questions were taken from previous exams and quizzes and there is a high likelihood that a significant number of them will appear on future exams and quizzes. They will give you a good feel for the type of questions that are used for testing in this class. Fourth, engage in what scientists call "active recall." There is considerable research in the educational and psychological literature on specifically what studying tactics work best for successful exam performance. Reading carefully, writing down unfamiliar terms and looking up their meanings, making outlines, and rereading material several times are all good strategies for learning. However, researchers are finding that a crucial element of learning is the following: Putting a book aside and hiding your notes, recalling everything you can, writing it down, and then saying it out loud. When students study on their own, "active recall" (e.g., recitation or use of flashcards and other self-quizzing techniques) is the most effective way to inscribe something in long-term memory

There are other things that students have found to be helpful such as studying in groups or getting tutors. These tactics, however, seem to be less important than the four "musts" I have mentioned above. When students perform poorly on exams it typically is due to their failure to execute one or several of the requirements stated above.

Students also ask me how much time they should be studying for an exam. The answer to this is of course highly variable. For some, it is only a few hours a day, while for others it is much more than this. If you are doing poorly, you clearly are not spending enough time on the material.

Having prepared diligently for the exam, you are now in a position to achieve success. Get a good nights rest and be in class on time. Bring your ID card with you (or your NY State driver's license) as well as three or four # 2 pencils. Also, have your 9 digit MyUalbany number memorized since you will need to reproduce it on the exam scantron sheet. Listen carefully when the test instructions are explained in class. I have had students in the past who have received a 0 on an exam since they failed to listen to the instructions.

Everything must be cleared from the top of your desk while taking an exam. Also, no hats can be worn and you are not permitted to speak to anyone. If you come late to an exam or quiz , we reserve the right to not allow you to take an exam or quiz.

You are not permitted to leave the class during the exam unless you receive permission from me or one of the proctors. If you have a question during the exam, you should raise your hand and someone will come around and try to help you. When you have completed the exam, you are allowed to leave after turning in your scantron sheet and your exam sheet and showing us your SUNY ID card or driver's license. Importantly, if you do not have identification (SUNY ID card or driver's license), you will receive a 0 on an exam or quiz.

Each exam that you take in this class consists of 60 multiple choice questions and true/false questions. Importantly, the questions are multiple choice and not "multiple guess." I do not wish to trick students or otherwise try to fool them by constructing questions that are difficult to interpret. As a general rule, I do not test students for their recall of names or dates. I am interested instead in your understanding of concepts and your ability to apply those concepts to every day life. You will be tested for your understanding of content, theory, and practical information, but you will also be assessed for your ability to translate that material into real life situations. A close examination of the practice exams will help you to understand exactly what I mean by this. Finally, none of the exams is cumulative. That is, you are only responsible for a set amount of information on each exam and you are not re-tested for understanding of that content on subsequent exams.

There is a definite successful strategy to test taking when exams consist of multiple choice questions. Usually, you can eliminate several answers for any question because they seem so outrageous. Then, you can decide on the suitability of the remaining answers. By eliminating answers, you can then devote your time and energy to other more suitable answers. This is good test taking strategy since you maximize the limited time you have available. You will have plenty of time to work on the exam and you are of course permitted to take the entire class period. However, it is unusual for students to take more than 50 minutes in completing multiple choice exams in my classes.

If there are questions that you find to be particularly perplexing, do not dwell upon them. Instead, eliminate an alternative answer and then move on. Come back to the question at the end but don't agonize over it unnecessarily. You are better off spending your time on what you know versus what you are not sure of. Once again, this is a wise test taking strategy since you are really maximizing your time on what you know as opposed to what can only be described as guess work.

I have noticed a tendency among students through the years to "over think" on certain questions and not go with their gut feelings. This tendency should be avoided. As stated earlier, I am not interested in providing trick questions to students. If you are having difficulty with a particular question it probably is due to you making it more complicated than it really is. Usually, your first reaction to a question will be the correct one.

You should note from the syllabus that your lowest exam score is dropped. I have done this for a very simple reason. Roughly 95% of my classes consist of freshman who are still adjusting to college life and my style of multiple choice exams. Many students in my classes in the past have not done well on the first or even second exam since they are still adjusting to my style of teaching and testing. Once they realize what they need to rectify in their studying habits, they soon begin doing well. I am sensitive to those adjustments that need to be made and I do not want to unnecessarily penalize students who are making some pronounced changes in their studying styles. Hence, by dropping the lowest exam score of each student, no one is being penalized for being in the middle of what can often be a difficult college adjustment period.

A few comments on cheating during tests are appropriate. Giving or receiving unauthorized help before, during, or after an exam constitutes cheating. Examples of unauthorized help include collaboration of any sort during an examination (unless specifically approved by the me); collaboration before an examination (when such collaboration is specifically forbidden by the me); use of notes, books, or other aids during an examination (unless permitted by me); arranging for another person to take an examination in one's place; looking upon someone else's examination during the examination period; intentionally allowing another student to look upon one's examination; the unauthorized discussing of test items during the examination period; and the passing of any examination information to students who have not yet taken the examination, and the use of Ipods and translation devices. There can be no conversation while an examination is in progress unless specifically authorized by me. The penalty for cheating on an examination in this class is a 0 for the exam. All of these statements regarding cheating on examinations are consistent with what is printed in the *Undergraduate Bulletin*.

I have witnessed just about everything in the years I have been teaching at the college level. From the "roving eyes" affliction to students giving American Sign Language (ASL) to each other from distant points in the classroom! Cheating demeans everyone and it is dealt with swiftly and severely in my classes. Some students who have cheated in my previous classes have received failures and others have even been suspended from school. Clearly, it is your choice as to how you want to conduct yourself but there is no sympathy at all for those who seek the easy, unethical route at SUNY-Albany.

One final note regarding examinations. You will see on the syllabus that they are scheduled for particular days and times. This does not change and it is in fact chipped in stone. Please do not come to me and request a special date to take an exam because you have "other commitments." The only permissible reason for rescheduling an exam is illness and you must have documentation from a physician and/or the dean to verify the fact that you could not make it to an exam. Any other non-medical reason must be sanctioned, documented and verified by the Dean of Undergraduate Studies. The penalty for unauthorized missing of exams is a 0 for the exam. Once again, I have heard every excuse imaginable for missing an exam.

From "I overslept" to "I have tickets for a flight to Cancun"....none of it is legitimate. This policy is consistent with what is seen in the *Undergraduate Bulletin*.

In addition to 4 tests, I also give 2 unannounced "pop" quizzes over the course of the semester. The material contained in the quizzes can come from material presented in class as well as assigned readings in the texts. The quizzes are comprehensive and can cover material from the beginning of the course through to the date of the quiz.

Lastly, it is your responsibility to be present in class to take tests and quizzes. Students can not take tests and quizzes in Psychology 101 classes that they are not formally enrolled in through the registrar's office. Thus, because I frequently teach several sections of Psychology 101 each semester, you will receive a 0 for a quiz or a test if you happen to take it in a section that you are not formally enrolled in through the registrar's office.

COMPLETING THE RESEARCH PARTICIPATION REQUIREMENT

In addition to the exams and quizzes, you will also be expected to complete the research participation requirement. Every student taking Psychology 101 must complete this requirement during the course of the semester. You have a rather lengthy handout which describes how to complete this requirement. I will not repeat that information here but what I will do is give you some advice which will help you to avoid some common pitfalls.

Psychology is a laboratory-based discipline and it is important that you have some exposure to the manner in which psychologists do research. You have three ways in which you can gain this kind of experience. You can participate as a subject in research, you can attend research colloquia, or you can write a short paper summarizing a particular area of research in psychology. Importantly, in the case of the third option, doing a short research paper, you must receive clearance from me on your tropic during the first 3 weeks of class. Please do not come to me during the last few weeks of class and tell me that you now wish to choose that option to fulfill the research participation requirement. I will simply tell you that it is no longer an option for you since you should have cleared the topic with my teaching assistant much earlier in the semester. The additional mechanics and details of completing the research participation requirement are presented in the handout you have received.

Every semester I give out incompletes to 20-30% of my introductory psychology students. The most frequent reason for this results from the fact that they simply did not read the research participation handout and/or they didn't take the information in it seriously. Importantly, a good portion of the incompletes automatically turn to Es when students fail to make up the required work.

In light of the large number of incompletes and resulting Es that emerge from introductory students not completing the research participation requirement, I have two pieces of very important advice to the students in my psychology 101 classes. First, read the handout very carefully and follow the instructions to the letter. Second, schedule your research participation work such that you are not scrambling at the end of the semester to finish up things that you should have completed earlier in the semester. If you follow this advice, then you will not be among the many students each year who either fail the course or must go through a great deal of bureaucratic red tape to get their grade changed.

CLOSELY MONITORING YOUR OWN PERFORMANCE

An important key to success in this class is your vigilance regarding your own performance. Students accumulate points in this class by way of performance on exams and quizzes. Let me discuss how you should monitor your performance in each of these areas.

After you take each exam or quiz in the class, your point totals are reported by the last four digits of your 9 digit myUalbany number. When you view this information, you will be able to see your point total as well as various statistics showing how the rest of the class performed. To get a quick read on how you stand in the class after each exam or quiz, all one needs to do is to take their point total and divide it by the top point total.

Importantly, this is just a way for you to monitor your progress in the course as you go along. I do not give out any letter grades in this class until the course has been completed. At that time, I add your points for exams and quizzes and then I distribute the grades usually on the basis of a modified normalized curve. Exam point totals usually account for about 70% of the course grade and quizzes usually account for about 30% of the course grade.

You are welcome to come to my office and view your exams and quizzes during my office hours. Whether you are doing well or you are doing poorly, it is always a good idea to see where you went wrong on a particular test. If you are not doing well on exams and quizzes, you should definitely make an appointment to come and see me so we can do some brainstorming about improvement. Each semester it is disappointing how few students, especially those that are not doing well, fail to check their exam scores and fail to come to see me if they are not doing well. Those poor performing students who do come to seek help often wait much too long to do so. A good rule of thumb is that you should come and see me soon after the first exam if you are not doing well.

GETTING HELP WHEN YOU NEED IT

My office hours are listed in the syllabus and you should never hesitate to come and see me during those times. There is no need to make an appointment. Simply come during my office hours and I will help you with whatever problems you are having. If my office hour times are not conducive to your schedule, I am sure that we can arrange another time that is mutually satisfactory.

I have some guidelines regarding my office hours that should be helpful to you and me to ensure that we make good use of our time. My office hours are specifically designed for the following purposes: (1) to help students understand text or lecture material that they are having difficulties with; (2) to discuss material in psychology that students find particularly intriguing; (3) to advise students with respect to future course work, graduate school, and potential careers in psychology; (4) to go over exams and quizzes with students; (5) to counsel students regarding improved performance on exams. Although I am a psychologist, my office hours are not for counseling you regarding personal or family problems you may be having. This is best accomplished by seeking aid at the Counseling Center on campus. Also, my office hours are not for any aspect of the research participation requirement. Any questions concerning this requirement should be directed toward my teaching assistant.

I am frequently contacted by telephone or email regarding exam and quiz performance information. Because I never know for sure who is on the other end, it is against university confidentiality policies to give out this kind of information in this manner. The best way to get this information is of course to monitor your performance by frequently checking your exam and quiz scores. Then, to the extent that you need additional help and information, you should come to me during my posted office hours listed in the syllabus.

SOME FINAL THOUGHTS

Everything you need for achieving success in this class is covered in *Learning About Psychology*. As the saying goes, "you can lead a horse to water but you can't necessarily make him drink." The same holds true for your ultimate level of achievement in this class. You have a roadmap for high achievement but you must now provide the motivation, the sweat, and the inspired work. Hopefully, you will follow the blueprint for success I have provided and you will combine it with your potential for doing well. I wish you success in your journey through psychology 101. The study of behavior is a fascinating topic and I hope to make it come alive for you in the days and weeks ahead!

Part II.   Lecture Outline

THE HISTORY OF PSYCHOLOGY

I.   *Is Psychology Necessary?*

II.   *How do We Define Psychology?*

A.   Important websites for learning about Psychology

Controversial Issue #1: Should Animals be Used in Psychological Research?

B. What is our behavior a product of?

III. The 4 Viewpoints of Psychology

A. Physiological/biological viewpoint

B. Intrapsychic viewpoint

C. Social/behavioral viewpoint

D. Holistic viewpoint

E. Conclusions

F. Controversy is the core of modern psychology

Controversial Issue #1: Should Animals be Used in Psychological Research?

IV.   *The Science of Psychology*

A. Philosophy--The roots of modern psychology

    1.   St. Augustine and Introspection

B. The evolution of two major approaches to the study of behavior

    1.   Faculty Psychology

        a.   Franz Gaul and Phrenology

    2.   Association Psychology

C. The founding of modern experimental psychology

      1. Wilhelm Wundt

    D. Other roots of contemporary psychology

V.   *Basic vs Applied Psychology*

A. Basic Science

B. Applied Science

METHODOLOGY IN PSYCHOLOGY

I. Why is Methodology so Important in Psychology

II. Important Terminology

A. Sample

B. Representative Sample

C. Random Sample

III. Data Gathering Techniques

A. Case Studies

B. Naturalistic observations

C. Surveys

D. Cross-cultural comparisons

E. Longitudinal/Cross-sectional studies

F. Laboratory based experiments

    1. Independent Variables

    2. Dependent Variables

    3. Experimental Groups

    4. Control Groups

    4. An Actual Experiment

       The Effects of THC on Sexual Behavior

IV. Experimental vs Correlational Research

A. What happens when a scientist can conduct a true experiment?

B. What is a correlation?

1. Strengths of correlations

2. Weaknesses of correlations

2. Examples of correlations

3. Important take home message about correlations

V. Methodological Problems and Solutions

A. Experimental bias

B. Self-fulfilling prophecy

1. Robert Rosenthall

a. Bloomer's Study

b. Maze Bright/Maze Dull Study

C. Double and single blind techniques in psychology

D. Measurement problems in psychology

GENES, HEREDITY, AND BEHAVIOR

I. **Evolutionary Psychology**

    A. Proximate causes of behavior

    B. Ultimate causes of behavior

    B. What is Evolutionary Psychology?

II. **Darwin and Evolution**

    A. Artificial selection

B. Natural selection

C. Reproductive success

    1. Variation

        a. Identical Twins vs Fraternal Twins

    2. Competition

III.   ***Humans and Natural Selection***

    A. Australopithecus

B. Homo habilis

C. Homo erectus

D. Homo sapiens

   1. bipedalism

   2. encephalization

IV.   ***Heredity and Genetics***

A. Basic Mendelian Genetics

B. Single gene traits

C. Polygenic traits

V.   *Studying Genes and Behavior*

A. Genetic disorders

1. PKU

2. Down's syndrome (Mongolism)

B. Artificial selection studies

   1. Tryon – Selection for intelligence in rats

   2. Cooper and Zubek---Impact of enriched environments

   3. Diamond and Rosenzweig – Impact of environment on the brain

B. Twin studies and concordance research

C. Controversial Issue #2: Does Genetic Testing Have Negative Psychological Effects?

THE BIOLOGY OF BEHAVIOR

I. Basic Neuroanatomy

A. The Famous Story of Phineus Gage

Sept 14th 1888 Phineus Gage working on a railway line as a dynamite specialist. Gage while Tamping the dynamite explodes sending the tamping iron pierced his skull. He survived the accident but his behavior radically changed. Went from serious, hardworking person to childish, whimsical, and silly. Established the brain (biological) basis for behavior.

B. Old brain (limbic system)

The limbic system is involved with basic emotional responses, Pain, Temperature, emotional responses (ex: sexual)

C. New brain (cerebral cortex)

involved with thinking, reasoning. A rather new evolutionary adaptation.

II. The Chemical Brain
Primary motor cortex - voluntary movement | Wernicke's area - speech understanding
Somatic sensory cortex - body sensations|

A. Basic anatomy and physiology of the neuron
. The human brain contains approximately 100 billion individual neurons

1. Cells of the Nervous System
. Human nervous system is comprised of Neurons & Glia, Neurons are involved with communication in the nervous system over short differences. The Glia provides the Neurons with nutrients
. Behavior depends upon the communication of neurons.

2. The Neuron - Building Block of Behavior

• <u>Soma</u> - cell body, • <u>Cytoplasm</u> - protects the cell, - <u>Axon</u> - where action potential begins ↳ Transmittion part of the neuron

• <u>Nodes of Ranvier</u> - involve the pushing from Myelin sheath (neuron impulses).

3. Afferent and Efferent Axons

• <u>Afferent Axon</u> - refers to bringing information into a structure.

• <u>Efferent Axon</u> - refers to carrying information away from a structure

4. The Action Potential

- The action potential, the firing of a neuron depends on two process:

a) Changes in the permeability of the cell membrane to sodium + potassium

b) changes in the polarity (charge) of the neuron.

5. The Synapse

s

6. The Post Synapse

7. Reuptake

Some neurotransmitters are sent back into terminal button

B.   Neurotransmitters and their function

1. Agonist and antagonist drugs

2. Serotonin (5-HT)

    a. Examples of changes in perceptual processing

3. Dopamine (DA)

    a. Parkinson's Disease

b. Schizophrenia

c. Runners high

d. Bliss

4. Oxytocin (OXY)

a. Maternal behavior in rats

  b. Reproductive behavior in voles

  c. Maternal aggression in mice

C. Neurotransmitters and human psychopathology

  1. Postpartum depression

  2. Other forms of psychopathology

  3. Aggression and hostility

LEARNING

I. History

A. Mentalism

B. Behaviorism

C. Definition of learning

1. Learning vs performance

II. Key Terminology

A. Reinforcement

1. Positive

3. Negative

B.   Punishment

C.   Can Positive Reinforcers have Negative Effects?

D.   Contiguity and reinforcement

E.   Conditioned reinforcement

III.   *Classical Conditioning*

A.   Twitmyer

B.   Pavlov

C.   Terminology (Basic Paradigm)

1. conditioned stimulus (CS)

2. unconditioned stimulus (UCS)

3. unconditioned response (UCR)

4. conditioned response (CR)

D. Basic factors influencing classical conditioning

1. Frequency of CS-UCS pairings

2. Duration of CS-UCS interval

3. Extinction

4. Temporal conditioning

5. Spontaneous Recovery

6. Stimulus generalization

7. Stimulus discrimination

8. Experimental neuroses

E.   Therapies based upon classical conditioning

1. The story of Albert and the white rat

2. Systematic desensitization/counterconditioning

   a.   Mary Cover Jones

   b.   Joseph Wolpe

3. Examples of Classical Conditioning in Real Life

4. Garcia experiment on conditioned taste aversion

    a. Practical applications

        1. Predator applications

        2. Treatment of breast cancer patients

5. Ader's experiment on conditioned immunosuppression

IV. *Operant Conditioning*

A.   Thorndike - cat in the puzzlebox

1. The learning curve

2. The law of effect

3. The law of exercise

B.   Koehler - Insight

C.   Skinner (Operant/Instrumental Conditioning)

1. Skinner's essential ingredients for learning

a. Motivation/suitable reinforcer

b. Structured environment

c. Specifying the terminal behavior

d. Shaping/successive approximations

3. Schedules of reinforcement and their effects on behavior

    a. CRF – Continuous reinforcement

    b. Schedules based upon the passage of Time (interval)

        1. Fixed Interval (FI)

2. Variable Interval (VI)

c. Schedules based upon the number of responses (ratio)

1. Fixed Ratio (FR)

2. Variable Ratio (VR)

4. Extinction

a. Partial reinforcement effect

b. Some real life examples

V. Comparisons between Operant and Classical Conditioning

A. James Olds -- Pleasure centers in the brain

B. Neal Miller -- Operant conditioning of involuntary responses

C. Behavioral Medicine/Biofeedback

D. Learned Helplessness

SENSATION AND PERCEPTION

I. **Hereditary Aspects of Sensation and Perception**

    A.   R.L. Fantz -- Recognition of human faces

    B.   Eleanor Gibson -- The visual cliff

II. **The Visual System**

    A.   Basic anatomy

    B.   Receptors for visual processing

        1. Rods -- black and white

2. Cones -- color

3. Two theories of color vision

    a. Trichromatic theory (Young-Helmholtz)

    b. Opponent-process theory

C.   Color blindness

D.   Visual illusions

1. Figure-ground relationships

2. Expectancy

E.   Vicary's work on subliminal perception

III.   *Olfaction*

A.   Basic anatomy -- lock and key receptor function

B.   Pheromones and animal behavior

1. Sex attractants

2. Maternal pheromones

3. Estrous synchrony

4. Puberty acceleration

5. Aggression promoting

C. The importance of olfaction for lower animal social behavior

D. The possibility of pheromonal communication in humans

    1. Russell - Maternal pheromones

    2. Russell – Tampon study

    3. Russell – Sweaty tee shirt study

        a. Miller and Manner "Scent of a Woman"

    4. McKlintock – Dormitory effect

5. Preti and Cutler – Underarm sweat and the dormiory

6. Michael – Aliphatic acids

7. Berliner and the "Feel Good" pheromone

IV. Reduction of Sensory Inputs

A. McGill sensory deprivation experiments

MEMORY

I. *The Stage Theory of Memory*

    A.   Sensory store

    B.   Short-term store

    C.   Long-term store

    D.   Evidence for the stage theory

        1.   Free recall studies/the Serial Position Curve

2. Clinical observations

3. Memory consolidation studies

II. The Search for the Engram

A. Karl Lashley searches for the engram

B. Richard Thompson and brain circuitry for simple responses

C. Early search for the engram 1950-1960

1. Halstead and Hayden – protein formation and memory

2. E Roy John - blocking memory with ribonuclease

3. Cameron – improving memory in senile patients

4. Memory consolidation studies

C.   Search for the engram, 1970-1980

1. MConnell's - cannibalistic transfer of memory in planaria

D.   Search for the engram, 1980 - 1990

1. Unger - scotophobin and memory

2. Jefferson – REM and memory

3. Agranoff – puromycin blockage of memory

4. Lynch - dendritic sprouting

5   Kandel – Long term potentiation

6   McGaugh – State Dependent Learning

CONSCIOUSNESS

I. **Laterality and the Split Brain**

    A. Functioning of the two cerebral hemispheres

        1. Corpus callosum

        2. Major hemisphere and its function

        3. Minor hemisphere and its function

    B. Sperry and Myers – The Split Brain - Corpus callosum cuts in cats

C. Split brain procedure in humans

    1. Two minds in the same body

II. *Sleep*

A. Important facts about sleep

    1. Sleep deprivation and mortality

    2. Walker Research on sleep disruption and memory

    3. Dinges research on chronic partial sleep deprivation

    4. Microsleeping

5. World famous accidents due to sleep impairment

6. Van Cauter research on sleep deprivation and health problems

7. McRobert and sleep derivation effects on sexual behavior

A.   Basics of the EEG machine

A.   EEG correlates of sleep

   1.   Basic parameters of electrical brain waves

         a. wave frequency

         b. wave amplitude

2.   Alpha waves

3.   Delta waves

4.   Kleitman and Dement – The Five Stages of Sleep

B.   Characteristics of REM Sleep

1.　　　Effects of REM deprivation

2.　　　REM and behavioral equilibrium

INTELLIGENCE AND INTELLIGENCE TESTING

I. **_What is Intelligence?_**

    a. Howard Gardner's 8 Types of Intelligence

        1. Logical – Mathematical

        2. Linguistic

        3. Naturalist

        4. Musical

        5. Spatial

        6. Bodily-Kinesthetic

7. Interpersonal

8. Intrapersonal

b. Sternberg and Practical Intelligence

1. Analytical

2. Practical

3. Creative

c. Theory of Emotional Intelligence

II. *History*

A.   Intelligence testing prior to formal intelligence tests

B.   Alfred Binet and the development of intelligence tests

    1.   Development of the first test

    2.   William Stern and the intelligence quotient (IQ)

    3.   Importation to the US - Lewis Terman and the Stanford-Binet

4. The WAIS and the WISC

5. The normal curve and IQ

III. **Nature, Nurture, and IQ**

A. Twin studies

1. Correlation coefficients explained

2. Identical twins vs fraternal twins

3. Correlation between parents and offspring

4.   Common genes or common environment

5.   Identical twins reared apart

B.   Can the environment influence IQ?

1.   Harold Skeels and the Iowa orphanage study

IV.   *Race and IQ*

A.   The research of Arthur Jensen

B.   IQ differences between blacks and whites

    1.   Controversial Issue #3: Is There a Racial Difference in IQ?

    2.   Why do African-Americans score lower than Caucasians?

        a. Unequal environments

        b. Unequal opportunities

        c. Culture bound tests

        d. Genetic differences

    3.   Research that shatters myths

a. IQs of black and interracial children adopted into white families

b. Gene structure in African-Americans and Caucasians

c. Lightness of skin color and IQ

d. Illegitimate children fathered by black and white servicemen

4.   Controversy over culture - free tests

5.   Concept of reaction range

DEVELOPMENT

I.   *Defining Development*

    A.   Quantitative changes

    B.   Qualitative changes

II.   *Qualitative Developmental Changes*

    A.   What it means to be a stage theorist

    B.   Jean Piaget - cognition

          I. Intelligence defined

2. Assimilation and accommodation

3. Stages of Intellectual Development

    a. Sensory motor period (percepts/object permanency)

    b. Pre-operational period (performing transformations)

    c. Concrete Operations

    d. Formal operations

C.   Sigmund Freud - Emotion

1. Id, ego, superego

2. The libido

3. Sources of gratification/sources of stimulation

4. Stages of emotional development

    a. Oral

    b. Anal

    c. Phallic

d. Latent

e. Genital

D. Harry Harlow and attachment behavior in primates

1.   Harlow's essential ingredients for attachment and love

a. Warmth

b. Contact comfort

c. Trust

2. Monster mothers and maternal rejection

3. Effects of prolonged social deprivation

4. Social deprivation and maternal behavior

5. Implications for human behavior

MOTIVATION

I.   *History and Background*

A.   Theories and definitions

1. The S-O-R motivation model

2. Motivation and intent

3. Drives and incentives

4. Primary drives and learned drives

5. Major defining characteristics of motivated behavior

a. Arousal

b. Direction

c. Desire

B.   Theories of Motivation

1. Pleasure-Pain principle

2. Reflex-Drive theories

3. Instinct theory

II.   *Hunger -- The Prototypical Motivation System*

A.   Schacter and studies of obesity

B.   External vs internal cues

C.   What are the signals for hunger

D.   Anorexia Nervosa

E.   Hypothalamic Feeding circuitry

F.   Stimulation and lesion studies

D.   Short-term controlling mechanisms

1.   Blood-sugar

2.   Stomach fullness

3.   Body temperature

E.   Long-term controlling mechanisms

    1.   Central mechanisms

    2.   Peripheral mechanisms

    3.   Appetitie hormones

III.   *Aggressive Behavior*

A.   Major characteristics of aggressive behavior

B.   Aggression: Nature or Nurture?

C.   Environmental determinants

D.   Controversial Issue #4: Does Viewing TV Increase a Child's Aggression?

E.   Controversial Issue #5: Does Porgnography Cause Men to Be Violent?

F.   Instinctual determinants

G.   Pain and aggression

H.   Frustration and aggression: The Dollard-Miller Hypothesis

G.   Biological determinants

       1.   The case of Charles Whitman

       2.   The Kleuver-Bucy Syndrome

       3.   Research by Jose Delgado implicating the limbic system

4.   Flynn's research on predatory and irritable aggression

5.   Testosterone and aggression

      a.   Intermale aggression in rodents

      b.   Testosterone and sex differences in the brain   (Gorski)

      c.   Sex difference in synapses (Raisman and Field)

      d.   Clinical syndromes

IV.   Sexual Behavior

A.   History

1. John Watson's unethical research

2. Sigmund Freud and the concept of the libido

4. Alfred Kinsey's groundbreaking survey work

5. Masters and Johnson's research leads the sexual revolution

a. The sexual response cycle

b. The new sex therapy

B.   Biological basis of sexual behavior

1. Sexual differentiation – Organization/Activation Theory

2. Masculinization/defeminization

3. Evidence for hormonal involvement

    a. Infrahuman primates and mammals
      1. Males
        a. Castration/testosterone replacement

        b. Hypothalamic modulation

c. Early testosterone effects

2. Females

    a. Cyclic nature of female sexual receptivity

    b. Ovariectomy/hormone replacement

    c. Hypothalamic control

    d. Early testosterone exposure

b. Humans

1. Males

    a. Variable effects of castration

    b. Hypogonadism

2. Females

    a. Premenopausal ovariectomy/menopause

    b. Adrenal testosterone

    c. Ovarian hormones modulate arousal

c. Sexual orientation

    1. Controversial Issue #6: Is Homosexuality Biological

        a. testosterone during puberty and adult life

b. Ward's prenatal stress studies

c. Dorner's prenatal stress study

d. Levay's research on homosexual brains

2. Lesbianism

a. Money and Ehrhard – Adrenogenital syndrome

b. Bailly and Pillard – concordance rate research

c. The famous case of John/Joan

PERSONALITY

I. *Theories of Personality*

A. Energy system approaches

1. Freud -- Psychoanalytic theory

a. History

b. Energy concepts

c. Subsystems of personality (id, ego, superego)

d. Ego defense mechanisms

1. Repression

2. Rationalization

3. Projection

4. Reaction Formation

5. Sublimation

6. Displacement

7. Denial

8. Regression

2. Jung -- Analytic theory

   a. Differences with Freud

   b. Personal Unconscious

   c. Collective Unconscious

   d. Introversion/Extroversion

B.   Behavioral system approach

    1.   Trait theories - Allport

        a. Common traits

        b. Individual traits

        c. Cardinal traits

        d. Central traits

        e. Secondary traits

    2.   Learning theories

        a. Bandura and the famous Bobo doll experiment

b. Rotter's concept of locus of control

C.   Self-actualization approaches

1.   Maslow's hierarchy of needs

a. Basic needs

b. Meta needs

c. Peak experiences

D.   Social system approach

1.   Harry Stack Sullivan and the social system approach

a. norms

b. roles

c. Role strain

d. The Self-System

II. Testing

A. Core concepts

1. Reliability

2. Validity

3. Norms

B. Insuring Reliability

1. Test-retest

2.   Internal

3.   Interjudge

C.   Insuring Validity

1.   Concurrent

2.   Predictive

3.   Content

III. *Personality Tests*

A. Personality inventories

  1. MMPI

    a. Development of a typical scale

    b. Different scales on the MMPI

      1. Depression

      2. Hypochondriasis

      3. Hysteria

      4. Psychopathic deviation

      5. Masculinity/Femininity

6. Paranoia

7. Psychasthenia

8. Schizophrenia

9. Mania

10. Social Introversion

B.   Projective tests

1.   General Characteristics

2.   Sentence completion

3.   Rorshach Inkblot

4.   TAT

ADJUSTMENT AND DISORDER

I.   *Defining Normality*

    A.   Medical science criteria

    B.   Psychological criteria

        1.   Statistical criterion

        2.   Ideal mental health criterion

        3.   Clinical criterion

C.   Problems in defining mental illness

       1. Thomas Szasz – The Myth of Mental Illness

       2. Controversial Issue #7: David Rosenhan – On Being Sane in insane Places: Do Diagnostic Labels Hinder Treatment

     1.   What do we mean by adjustment?

     2.   Decisions on maladjusted behavior

II.   *The Diagnostic and Statistical Manual (DSM)*

A.   The Five Axes of the DSM

1. Clinical Disorders

2. Personality Disorders and Mental Retardation

3. General Medical Condition

4. Psychosocial and Environmental Problems

5. Global Assessment of Functioning

A.   Neuroses

1.   Phobias

2.   Obsessions/compulsions

3.   Hysteria

B.   Psychoses

     1.   Schizophrenia

          a. Simple

          b. Hebephrenic

c. Catatonic

d. Paranoid

2.   Affective Reactions

a. Manic

b. Depressive

C.   Personality disorders

    1.   Antisocial Personality

    2.   Sexual deviance

D.   Organic based disorders

    1.   Melancholia

    2.   Stroke related disorders

3.   Senile psychoses

4.   Alzhiemers disease

5.   Venereal disease

6.   Alcohol addiction disorder

7.   Manic Depression

8.   Schizophrenia

III. *Epidemiology of Mental Disorder*

A. Demographic variability

    1. Gender

    2. Age

    3. Marital status

    4. Social class

5. Cross cultural variability

6. Ethnic group

TREATMENT OF MENTAL DISORDER

I.   The History of Treatment

      A.   Historical antecedents

      B.   Middle ages

      C.   Institutional approaches in Europe

      D.   Phillipe Pinel and dramatic changes in treatment

E.   Moral care in the United States

F.   Custodial care in the United States

G.   The advent of tranquilizers and antidepressants

H.   The therapeutic community and Max Jones

I.   Community Mental Health Programs and Half way houses

II.   *Major Forms of Therapy*

    A.   Physiological therapies (Biomedical)

        1.   Electroconvulsive shock therapy

        2.   Psychosurgery

        3.   Drug therapy

4. Controversial Issue #8: Are Drugs Really Effective in Treating Psychological Disorders?

a. Tranquilizers

b. Antidepressants

c. Antipsychotics

d. Hormone Therapies

4.   Three Issues in Drug Treatments

      a. Side Effects

      b. Use of Herbs

      c. Symptom Removal

B.   Intrapsychic therapy (Insight)

1.   Psychoanalytic therapy of Freud

2.   Humanistic therapy of Maslow and Rogers

3.   Rational Emotive Therapy (Ellis)

4.   Effectiveness of Insight Therapies – The Eysenk Report

5.   Factors influencing the effectiveness of insight therapies

C. Social/Behavioral therapy

1. Group therapy

a. Formal

b. Inspirational

c. Psychodrama

d. Transactional analysis

e.   Encounter groups

f.   Does Group Therapy Work?

2.   Milieu therapy

a.   Aversion therapy

b.   Systematic desensitization

a.   Token economies

SOCIAL PSYCHOLOGY

I. *Classic Experiments in Social Psychology*

    A. Methods in Social Psychology Experiments

        1. Ethics of deception

        2. Risk vs Reward

        3. Use of Stooges/Confederates

    B. The Evolution of Social Psychology Experiments

        1. Kurt Lewin and leadership styles

        2. Solomon Asch and conformity

    C. Stanley Milgram (Obedience)

1   Classic experiment

2.   Variations on classic experiment

        a.   Experimenter giving phone commands

        b.   Type of feedback from learner

        c.   Social support for disobedience

3.   Importance of Milgram's research

C.   The ethics of Milgram's Work

III. Selected Key Slides

Psychology 101 – Part I

- **Science of Psychology**

- **Biology of Behavior**

What is Psychology?

- Psychology is the scientific study of human behavior. The primary aim of psychology is to predict and control behavior.

The Four Viewpoints of Psychology

- The Physiological/Biological Viewpoint
  - (Dispositional factors)

  - Your biochemistry control your feelings, emotions and your personality

  - Your body exercises complete control over your mind

The Four Viewpoints of Psychology

- The Intrapsychic Viewpoint

  - Conscious and unconscious portions of your personality influence your behaivor

  - Your mind controls your body

The Four Viewpoints of Psychology

- The Social/Behavioral Viewpoint
  - (Situational factors)

  - Your thoughts, personality, behaviors are a product of the environment

The Four Viewpoints of Psychology

- **The Holistic Viewpoint**

  - **Physiological/Biological**
  - **Intrapsychic**
  - **Social/Behavioral**

Conclusion

- We use the same rigorous tools of scientific inquiry as physics, chemistry, and biology

- The use of modern technology allows us to study behavior from an interdisciplinary perspective

- We are just touching the tip of the iceberg in terms of what we really know about what our behavior is a product of!

Controversial Issue #1: Should Animals Be Used in Psychological Research

- Yes, they should
  - This research has played an extremely important role in improving the human and animal condition
  - There are elaborate federal regulations and professional guidelines that protect animals
  - Society has made the collective judgment that the benefits derived from animal research far outweigh the costs
  - Animals have played a pivotal role in improving the human condition and, in return, society should strive to treat them well

Controversial Issue #1: Should Animals Be Used in Psychological Research

- No, they should not
  - People who give basic rights to humans deny them to animals. Who is to judge? Why are humans making these moral distinctions? Specism
  - Many species are not covered by the Animal Welfare Act (insects and rodents)
  - The benefits of animal research are sometimes uncertain. We simply don't know what the outcome of a particular experiment may be. The cost to the animal is real...usually death

The Evolution of Two Major Approaches to the Study of Behavior

- Faculty Psychology

  - Franz Gall and Phrenology

  - The mind has a few principle inborn faculties such as thinking, feeling, and willing that account for all its activities

The Evolution of Two Major Approaches to the Study of Behavior

- Association Psychology

  - The content of the mind is limited to ideas coming to it by way of the senses

The Founding of Modern Experimental Psychology

- In 1879, Wilhelm Wundt establishes the first Experimental Psychology Laboratory in Leipzig, Germany

- The <u>quantification</u> of behavior

An Important Distinction: Basic Versus Applied Science

- <u>Basic Research:</u> Knowledge is acquired for its own sake to satisfy a basic curiosity. The immediate usefulness of that information is not considered

- <u>Applied Research:</u> Taking the findings of basic research and using them to accomplish a practical

Why is Methodology so Important in the Discipline of Psychology?

- Most people are considerably more interested in what psychologists have to say in contrast to how they find it out.

- You must view the importance of methodology in psychology as being similar to learning the rules of a football or basketball game.

- Inappropriate methodology can lead to erroneous conclusions

Methodology

- <u>Sample:</u> A portion (a part of) the total number of individuals that could be selected

- <u>Representative Sample:</u> A sample that is of sufficient size to reflect the universe of all possible individuals

- <u>Random Sample:</u> A sample in which every person in the universe of relevant individuals has an equal chance of being selected

The Case Study

- An in intensive investigation of one or a few individuals with respect to a single psychological phenomena

- The case of <u>hysteria</u> studied by Sigmund Freud

- Case studies provide for an in depth, descriptitve analysis of a few individuals. But because so few individuals are studied, the results may not generalize to

Naturalistic Observations

- Studying behavior as it occurs in its natural habitat. The experimenter never interferes with what is going on

- Jane Goodall and her important field observations on primates

- Naturalistic observations help us to understand behavior as it naturally occurs. But determining what causes behavioral change can be a challenge

Surveys

- A survey collects information about attitudes and behaviors. They can be written or oral

- Kinsey's famous sexual attitudes survey

- The Literary Digest survey of 1936

- Survey's are powerful instruments for assessing behavior in large numbers of individuals. But the samples used must be representative of the universe of all possible individuals.

Cross Cultural Comparisons

- Comparing the behavior of people who reside in dramatically different cultures

- Margaret Meade's famous cross cultural comparison of the behavior of Samoan people

- Cross cultural comparisons help us to establish whether or not the factors that control behavior can be generalized to people from all cultures

- Takes a lot of time and resources

Longitudinal/Cross Sectional Studies

- Longitudinal studies examine how behavior changes with age.

- The famous Wisconsin Longitudinal Study (WLS) has examined the behavior and attitudes of 15,000 Wisconsin residents every 5 years starting back in 1957 when they graduated from high school.

- Longitudinal studies are expensive to conduct and take a very long time to complete. They are often conducted in conjunction with cross sectional assessments

The Laboratory Based Study

- In a laboratory based experiment, the scientist:

  - holds all variables constant except one (called the treatment variable) which is allowed to systematically change

  - observes the effects of the treatment variable on behavioral responses

Key Components of a Laboratory Based Experiment

- Variables: Any factor capable of change

  - Independent variable: The one variable that an experimenter allows to systematically change while keeping all others constant

  - Dependent variable: The variable that the experimenter expects will change. In psychology, it is typically a behavioral response

Key Components of a Laboratory Based Experiment

- Experimental Group
  - That group of randomly selected subjects that is exposed to the experimental treatment

- Control Group
  - That group of randomly selected subjects that is exposed to everything that the experimental group is exposed to with the exception of the treatment

An Actual Laboratory Based Experiment

- Examining the effects of the psychoactive component of marijuana (THC) on the sexual behavior of mice

- Advantages: Cause and effect can be determined

- Disadvantages: The situation is so over controlled that it may bear no relationship to an organism in its natural habitat

What Happens When A Scientist Can't Conduct An Experiment?

- <u>Hypothesis</u>: Normal visual development depends not only on physical maturation but on visual experience.

    - Raise babies in total darkness?

    - Experiment with animals (e.g., cats)

    - People who have been born blind and were later able to see through corrective surgery

What Happens When A Scientist Can't Conduct An Experiment With Animals?

- <u>Hypothesis</u>: The ability to hear spoken language is necessary for normal language development.

    - Examine language development in subjects born with different degrees of deafness (e.g., conduct a correlational study to look at degrees of deafness (e.g., 10%, 30%, 50%, 70%) and language development).

Correlational Studies

- **What is a Correlation?**

    - **The tendency of two events to vary, be associated, or occur together in a way not expected on the basis of chance alone**

    - <u>**Correlations do not necessarily indicate causality**</u>

Misinterpreting Correlations

- Over a 2 week period of time in July, examine the relationship between the number of popsicles bought and consumed at Jones Beach and the number of people admitted to surrounding hospitals with heat stroke

- <u>Results</u>: On days that are warm, many popsicles are sold and many people are admitted to surrounding hospitals with heat stroke.

- <u>Conclusion</u>: Consumption of popsicles causes heat stroke

Some Methodological Problems

- **The <u>self-fulfilling prophecy</u> and how <u>expectations</u> can influence the outcome of psychological experimentation**

    - Robert Rosenthal studies

        - Bloomers study

        - Maze bright – maze dull study

    - Double blind Technique

Problems of Measurement

- **Thinking that you are manipulating a variable when in fact you are not**

    - e.g., Learn while you sleep studies

Key Concepts in Understanding Genes, Heredity and Behavior

- **What do we mean by proximate causes of behavior?**

    – The immediate day to day environmental factors or stimuli that influence our responses

Key Concepts in Understanding Genes, Heredity and Behavior

- **What do we mean by ultimate causes of behavior?**

    – How past environmental conditions, sometimes occurring over many generations, can shape our behavior

Key Concepts in Understanding Genes, Heredity and Behavior

- **What is evolutionary psychology?**

    – It is the study of how an organism's long term history has contributed to behavioral adaptation

Key Concepts in Darwinian Evolutionary Theory

- **Artificial selection**

    – Selecting some animals to breed but not others based upon specific desirable characteristics

Key Concepts in Darwinian Evolutionary Theory

- **Natural selection**
    – Organisms reproduce differentially. Within any given population some members will produce more offspring than others

    – An animal that possesses a characteristic that helps it to survive or adapt to changes in the environment is likely to live longer and to produce more offspring than are animals that do not have this characteristic

Key Concepts in Darwinian Evolutionary Theory

- **Reproductive success**

    – The ability of an animal to produce offspring defines that animals reproductive success

    – The number of viable offspring it produces relative to the number of viable offspring produced by other members of the same species

Key Concepts in Darwinian Evolutionary Theory

- **Variation**

  - Animals differ in both physical and behavioral characteristics

- **What is responsible for variation?**

  - Genes
  - Environment

Key Concepts in Darwinian Evolutionary Theory

- **Competition**

  - Individuals of a given species share the same environment therefore they compete for food, mates, territory

Genes Regulate Development and Behavior Through the Production of New Proteins

- **Single gene** effects (e.g., hair color, eye color)

- **Polygenic** effects (e.g., behaviors like running, and complex behavioral

Genetic Disorders: Phenylketonuria (PKU)

- A single gene defect
- There are thousands of genes on each chromosome and it is the absence of one of them that results in this syndrome
- Children afflicted with PKU show extremely low IQs, light pigmentation, shorter stature, elevated irritability
- Appear normal at birth but deteriorate rapidly in terms of intelligence

Genetic Disorders: Phenylketonuria

- **Phenylalanine** is a protein found in many dairy products.

- The defective gene causing PKU prevents a person from converting the substance phenylalanine (a protein) into other proteins.

- Phenylalanine buildup becomes toxic to the CNS and causes progressive retardation.

- Remedy: Low phenylalanine diets

Genetic Disorders: Down's Syndrome (Mongolism)

- 1 of every 600 births
- Severely retarded with few exceptions
- IQ usually below 50
- Eyelids superficially resemble those of an oriental
- Short, stubby fingers
- Small ears
- Protruding tongues

Genetic Disorders:
Down's Syndrome (Mongolism)

- <u>Karyotyping</u> (photographing) of chromosomes first became available in 1959

- It shows that all Down's Syndrome kids have an extra chromosome on the 21st pair

- Down's Syndrome children have 47 instead of the normal compliment of 46 chromosomes

Genetic Disorders
Down's Syndrome: Mongolism

- A doctor can remove fetal cells from the amniotic fluid surrounding the fetus and karyotype the cells. This is called <u>amniocentesis</u>

Controversial Issue # 2:
Does Genetic Testing Have Negative Psychological Effects?

- Increasingly psychology is showing that behavioral problems may be linked to our genetic makeup:
  - Aggression and violence...XYY condition
  - Attention deficit disorder (ADD)
  - Alcoholism
  - Manic depression (bipolar disorder)

Controversial Issue # 2:
Does Genetic Testing Have Negative Psychological Effects?

- <u>Reasons for testing</u>:

  - Earlier prevention treatment

  - The benefits of knowing about one's genes may outweigh the risks

  - Patients and their spouses realize that psychological disorders are not 100% heritable

Controversial Issue # 2:
Does Genetic Testing Have Negative Psychological Effects?

- <u>Reasons against testing</u>:

  - Genetic testing may actually increase a person's risk of mental illness (the self-fulfilling prophecy)

  - Genetic testing could cause stress, worry, and even suicidal preoccupation

  - Genetic testing for psychological disorders is not as sure as genetic testing for physical disorders

  - Once genetic testing is done, the knowledge can never be undone

Controversial Issue # 2:
Does Genetic Testing Have Negative Psychological Effects?

- There are good reasons for and against people submitting to genetic testing

- <u>Thought question</u>: Assume that it has just been discovered that you have a close family member that has been found to be schizophrenic. Would you submit to genetic testing to examine whether or not you possessed the genes for

The Cells of the Nervous System

- The human nervous system is comprised of two kinds of cells:
  - Neurons
  - Glia

- The human brain contains approximately 100 billion individual neurons.

- Behavior depends upon the communication between neurons.

Cells of the Nervous System

- Terms used to describe the neuron include the following:

  - <u>Afferent axon</u> - refers to bringing information into a structure.

  - <u>Efferent axon</u> - refers to carrying information away from a structure.

Our Brain: A Giant Chemical Factory Some Common Neurotransmitters

- Serotonin (5-HT)
- Dopamine (DA)
- Acetylcholine
- Epinephrine
- Norepinephrine
- Endorphin
- Oxytocin (OXY)
- Adrenalin
- Noradrenalin
- Vasopressin

Drugs Can Change How Neurotransmitters Function

- <u>Agonists</u> are drugs that *facilitate* the effects of a particular neurotransmitter on the postsynaptic cell

- <u>Antagonists</u> are drugs that *oppose or inhibit* the effects of a particular neurotransmitter on the postsynaptic cell

Examples of Agonist and Antagonist Drugs

- <u>L-Dopa</u> is a drug agonist that facilitates the synthesis of dopamine

- <u>Reserpine</u> is a drug antagonist that inhibits the storage of norepineprhine in synaptic vesicles

- <u>PCPA</u> is a drug antagonist that inhibits the synthesis of serotonin

- <u>Cocaine</u> is a drug agonist that blocks dopamine reuptake

The Serotonergic System

- Serotonin (5-HT)… the workhorse neurotransmitter of the brain
  - Involved in mood, appetite, violence, aggression

- Serotonin acts in many areas…but is most involved in the frontal lobes and the thalamus

- Thalamus is the principle gateway for all sensory information to the cortex of the brain. It is like a giant valve

- Serotonin can influence how the frontal cortex makes decisions

Serotonin in Japanese Religious Pilgrims

Following isolation, Japanese religious pilgrims experience a dramatic increase in serotonin receptors on red blood cells. This is associated with distorted perceptions and hallucinations

LSD Binds on Serotonin Receptors

Visionary artists use LSD as a tool to move beyond their ordinary perceptions to states of consciousness they would not ordinarily experience. LSD is known to bind with serotonin receptors and overload the brain

Parkinson's Disease: Dopamine Deficiency in the Basal Ganglia

In Parkinson's disease, cells in the brain that produce dopamine begin to degenerate. Less dopamine gets to the basal ganglia, thus compromising smooth and controlled movements.

The Dopamine Theory of Schizophrenia

The "dopamine theory of schizophrenia" states that schizophrenia is caused by an overactive dopamine system in the brain.

Dopamine, Endorphin and Runner's High

- Dopamine can regulate pain in our body. When there is a physical injury, the neurotransmitter endorphin is released.

- Endorphin (also called endogenous opioids) binds on special receptor sites in the brain that shuts off neurons and allows more dopamine to be secreted into the frontal lobe

Dopamine and Bliss

- The "love potent" of dopamine and noradrenalin are secreted at high levels in the infatuation stage of a relationship.

- There is a sudden "rush" of these neurotransmitters in the brain.

- Sweaty palms, racing heart, flushed cheeks…these area all behaviors that can accompany love.

- The more primitive part of the brain (the limbic system) can therefore override the logic exhibited by the

Understanding Human Psychopathology

- Some reports suggest that vasopressin and oxytocin receptors may be altered in:
  - autism
  - Tourette's syndrome
  - Alzheimer's disease
  - schizophrenia

Emil Coccaro's Work on Prozac and Road Rage

- Low levels of serotonin are associated with high levels of aggression

- Using the drug Prozac (an anti-depressant), Carcaro has had success in lowering aggression in people that have a very short fuse and are constantly getting into trouble

- Prozac increases levels of serotonin in the brain. It seems to diminish impulsive behavior and angry outbursts

Psychology 101 – Part II

- **Learning and Behavior Analysis**

- **Sensation and Perception**

- **Memory and Consciousness**

Behaviorism

- Led by Clark Hull, B.F. Skinner and John Watson

- It is impossible to study behavior scientifically by <u>subjective</u> reports.

- Psychology must concentrate on <u>objective</u> analysis of observable behavior

Distinguishing Learning from Performance

- <u>Performance</u>---What an organism actually does

- <u>Learning</u>---A relatively permanent change in behavior that is due to experience with the environment

Types of Reinforcers: Postive Reinforcers

- **Any stimulus whose presentation leads to the strengthening of responses that came before it**
  – **Example**
    - **Giving candy to a young child for good behavior**

Types of Reinforcers: Negative Reinforcement

- A stimulus whose withdrawal increases the liklihood of a response that led to the termination of an aversive stimulus

- Example
  - A rat terminating shock when it runs to the end of a straight alley
  - Violin players in an orchestra changing the way they play when they see that there conductor is not pleased with how they play

Punishment

- A stimulus whose presentation leads to the reduction of the response that came before it

- Example

  - A child being spanked by a parent for disruptive behavior
  - A rat receiving shock when it depresses a bar to receive food

Can Positive Reinforcers Have Negative Effects?

- Powerful positive reinforcers like alcohol and addictive drugs like heroin and cocaine can have devastating effects.

- Addicted individuals will engage in antisocial and illegal behaviors to obtain these drugs.

- The addict will neglect many other healthy behaviors in order to obtain drugs

Contiguity and Reinforcement

- Contiguity is the closeness in time between two events.

- Reinforcement (R) is most effective when it is delivered contiguous (close in time) with a behavioral response

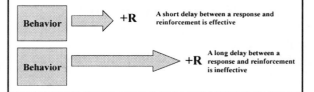

| Behavior | ⇒ | +R | A short delay between a response and reinforcement is effective |

| Behavior | ⇒ | +R | A long delay between a response and reinforcement is ineffective |

Conditioned Reinforcers

- Reinforcers may satisfy basic biological needs like
  - warmth
  - sex
  - hunger
  - thirst
  - removal of pain

- Reinforcers are <u>not</u> always related to satisfying basic biological needs.

- Money, a smile, praise, school grades, peer approval..are CONDITIONED REINFORCERS because they are associated with basic reinforcers

The Discovery of Classical Conditioning

- <u>E.B. Twitmyer</u>, a neurologist at the University of Pennsylvania, was the actual discoverer of classical conditioning

- A subject whose knee was struck with a rubber hammer many times, and a warning bell was sounded each time the hammer was dropped, resulted in the subject responding to the bell alone by exhibiting the knee jerk (patellar) response

Ivan Pavlov, A Giant in Psychology

- Pavlov 1849-1936

- Medical school training

- Research in physiology

- Studied the physiology of the digestive process

- Won the Nobel prize in 1904 for his work on salivation and gastric function

- Initially was not interested in the study of behavior

Key Factors Influencing Conditioning: Frequency of Pairings

- The more times the CS is paired with the UCS, the greater the liklihood that conditioning will take place

  5 pairings of CS + UCS = Little or no conditioning

  100 pairings of CS + UCS = Strong conditioning

The Classical Conditioning Paradigm in Pavlov's Dogs

I.   UCS   ⟹   UCR
        (meat powder)   (salivation)

II.   Neutral stimulus + UCS   ⟹   UCR
           (bell)   (meat powder)   (salivation)

III.   CS   ⟹   CR
        (bell)   (salivation)

Key Factors Influencing Conditioning: Temporal Factors

- Conditioning is best when the CS is presented immediately before the UCS. If the CS is long before or after the UCS, learning does not occur

  CS .5 seconds before   UCS = Strong conditioning

  CS several minutes before UCS = Little or no conditioning

  UCS before CS = Little or no conditioning

Key Factors Influencing Conditioning: Extinction

- Conditioned responses can be unlearned very rapidly. If the CS alone is presented many times without the UCS, the response will extinguish

Presentation of CS Alone after many CS-UCS pairings produces a robust CR

Repeated presentation of CS Alone produces a weak CR

Repeated presentations of CS Alone eventually produces no CR (Extinction)

Key Factors Influencing Conditioning: An Extinguished Response is Not Forgotten

- An extinguished response is not completely forgotten. Relearning proceeds much quicker than original learning

Key Factors Influencing Conditioning: The Passage of Time Can Serve as a CS

- Time alone can be a conditioned stimulus

Key Factors Influencing Conditioning: Spontaneous Recovery

- Returning an organism to a place where it has been conditioned will result in reappearance of the behavior in the absence of explicit stimuli

Example of Stimulus Generalization

- A child bitten by a large dog.
  - On future occasions a small dog might be just as scary to the child

- When a predator makes a slightly different sound or is seen from a different angle, its prey can still respond quickly

Stimulus Discrimination

- An organism learns to respond to one stimulus and not another

+ Means reinforcement
- Means no reinforcement

Example of Stimulus Discrimination

- At an intersection

  - Light turns red and you take your foot off of the accelerator and place it on the brake

  - Light turns green and you take your foot off the brake and place it on the

Experimental Neurosis

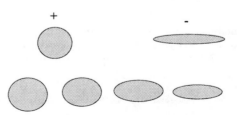

- Pavlov found that he could create experimental neurosis in dogs through a simple discrimination procedure

Therapies Based on Classical Conditioning

- Mary Cover Jones and Counter-Conditioning

  - You can't give two incompatible responses to the same CS (i.e., it is not possible to feel both fearful and pleasurable at the same time)

  - Attach a response other than fear to the CS

Watson and Little Albert

- Watson sounded a loud noise when little Albert was playing with a white rat.

- Albert was startled and began to cry

- On future occasions when Albert saw a white rat he began to cry and was fearful

- In addition to the rat, all fury objects (stimulus generalization produced fear (conditioned fear) in Albert

Therapies Based on Classical Conditioning

- Joseph Wolpe and Systematic Desensitization

In an airplane flying

Seated and ready for takeoff

Boarding an airplane

Getting boarding pass at gate

Parking car at airport

Driving to airport

Packing in preparation for flight

Purchasing airline ticket

Looking at pictures of an airplane in flight

Hierarchy of Fears

**A common phobia:
Fear of flying**

Classical Conditioning in Real Life

- The toilet flush phenomena

- Reduced moisture in the winter and static electricity

- Opening a can of cat food

- Method acting (Stanislavsky) and memories of early (sad) emotional experiences

Conditioned Taste Aversion

CS   +   UCS ⟹ UCR

Taste/smell of gum)   (Nausea)   (Vomiting and disgust)

CS ⟹ CR

Taste of gum)   (Vomiting and disgust)

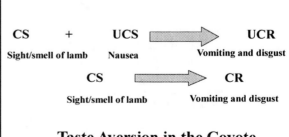

CS   +   UCS ⟹ UCR

Sight/smell of lamb   Nausea   Vomiting and disgust

CS ⟹ CR

Sight/smell of lamb   Vomiting and disgust

Taste Aversion in the Coyote

Conditioned Elevation of the Immune System

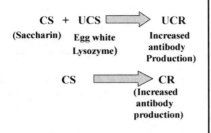

CS + UCS → UCR
(Saccharin) (Egg white Lysozyme) (Increased antibody Production)

CS → CR
(Increased antibody production)

Thorndike's Laws of Learning

- <u>Law of Exercise</u>: Stimulus response (S-R) connections are strengthened by practice

- <u>Law of Effect</u>: Stimulus response (S-R) connections are strengthened by reward

Wolfgang Kohler and Insight Learning

- Kohler believed that animals are intellectually capable of much greater feats than simple trial and error learning

- His research suggested that chimpanzees are capable of "insight" learning, the rapid perception of relationships

Skinner's Essential Ingredients for Learning

- Establish a level of motivation

- Specify the terminal response

- Use a highly structured environment

- Use successive approximations

Schedules of Reinforcement

- Continuous reinforcement (CRF)
- Two basic types of schedules that reflect how we really learn:

  - Interval schedules are based upon the passage of time
    - Fixed interval (FI)
    - Variable interval (VI)

  - Ratio schedules are based upon the number of responses that an organism exhibits
    - Fixed ratio (FR)
    - Variable ratio (VR)

Schedules of Reinforcement

- <u>Continuous reinforcement (CRF)</u>: Reinforcement for every response of the correct type

- <u>Fixed interval (FI)</u>: Reinforcement for the first response after a given delay since the previous reinforcement

- <u>Variable interval (VI)</u>: Reinforcement for the first response that follows an unpredictable delay (varying around a mean value) since the previous reinforcement

- <u>Fixed ratio (FR)</u>: Reinforcement following the completion of a set number of responses

- <u>Variable ratio (VR)</u>: Reinforcement for an unpredictable number of responses that varies around a mean value

Effects of Schedules of Reinforcement on Behavior

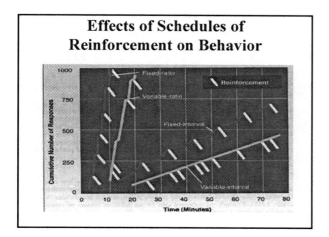

The Partial Reinforcement Effect (PRE)

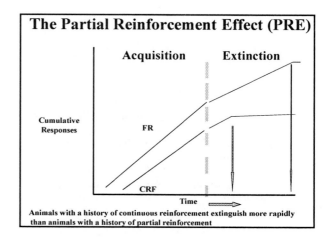

Animals with a history of continuous reinforcement extinguish more rapidly than animals with a history of partial reinforcement

Examples of Schedules of Reinforcement

- **Fixed Interval (FI)**
  - Tests given at regular intervals
    - Example: test administered every 4 weeks in a 16 week semester

Examples of Schedules of Reinforcement

- **Variable Interval (VI)**
  - Example: Pop quizzes

Examples of Schedules of Reinforcement

- **Fixed Ratio (FR)**
  - piece work in factory

Examples of Schedules of Reinforcement

- **Variable Ratio (VR)**
  - Gambling behavior

Comparing Two Types of Learning

Operant Conditioning	Classical Conditioning
• Voluntary responses	• Involuntary responses
• Emitted responses	• Elicited responses
• Responses shaped by reinforcement	• Reinforcement not needed (contiguity only)
• O learns how to operate on E	• E operates on O
• Involvement of cortex and higher brain areas	• Involvement of lower brain areas

Research Question

• Is it possible to operantly condition an involuntary response?

Shaping of Heart Rate

• **Neal Miller's research:**
  – Immobilized rats with curare preventing them from exhibiting voluntary responses

  – modified heart rate by giving rewarding brain stimulation to the medial forebrain bundle

• **Implications of Miller's research**
  – it is possible to operantly condition an involuntary response

  – it provided the groundwork for the field of behavioral medicine.

Learned Helplessness

Psychologist Martin Seligman discovered that animals with a history of exposure to inescapable shock failed to learn an avoidance response. Instead they learned to be helpless.

Seligman theory of learned helplessness is now one of the most prominent theories of how depression develops in humans.

Vision

• The vertebrate retina consist of two kind of receptors:

1. Rods - most abundant in the periphery of the eye and respond to faint light. (120 million per retina)

2. Cones - most abundant in and around the fovea. (6 million per retina)

   • Essential for color vision & more useful in bright light.

Two Theories of Color Vision

• **Trichromatic theory** (Young-Hemholtz Theory) suggests that we perceive color through the relative rates of response by three types of cones...each kind maximally sensitive to a different set of wavelengths.

  – Long wavelength cone: responds well to red or yellow

  – Medium wavelength cone: responds best to green and less to yellow

  – Short wavelength cone: responds best to blue

Two Theories of Color Vision

- The <u>opponent-process theory</u> suggests that we perceive color in terms of paired opposites.

  - The brain has a mechanism that perceives color on a continuum from red to green and another from yellow to blue.

  - A possible mechanism for the theory is that bipolar cells are excited by one set of wavelengths and inhibited by another.

Are Subliminal Visual Stimuli Effective in Changing Behavior?

- Subliminal visual stimuli go to lower brain areas but not to conscious areas of the cortex

- Subliminal stimuli can influence your behavior <u>but only if</u>:

  - All other sensory inputs must be greatly reduced or eliminated

  - You are motivated to make use of even weak hunches

What are Pheromones?

Chemical substances within species which, when they become gaseous, and are detected by other species members, can signal:

- sexual receptivity
- danger
- territorial boundaries.

Examples of Pheromones in Lower Animals

- Sex attractants in gypsy moths

- Maternal pheromone in rats

- Estrous synchrony pheromone in mice

- Puberty acceleration pheromone in mice

- Aggression promoting pheromone in mice

Olfaction is Extremely Important for Social Behavior in Lower Animals

- Olfactory bulb removal and ZNSO(4) treatments make animals anosmic (e.g., they lose the ability to smell). This suppresses:

  - Aggression

  - Maternal Behavior

  - Mating

Key Experiments in the Human Pheromone Story

- Russell: Maternal Pheromone

Infants prefer the breast pads of their mother in contrast to those worn by another mother

Key Experiments in the Human Pheromone Story

- **Russell:** Tampon Study

Males prefer the odors from females that are ovulating versus those that are not

Key Experiments in the Human Pheromone Story

- **Russell:** sweaty tee-shirt studies
  (estratetranol and androstadienone)

  – Females prefer the odors of males when they are ovulating but not when they are not ovulating

Key Experiments in the Human Pheromone Story

- McKlintock: Dormitory Effect

- Once females have lived together in a college dormitory for a few months their reproductive cycles become synchronized

Key Experiments in the Human Pheromone Story

- Preti and Cutler:

- Underarm Sweat may be responsible for the Dormitory Effect

Key Experiments in the Human Pheromone Story

- Michael: Vaginal Aliphatic Acids

- These acids are the sex attractant in the vaginal washings of baboons. Males are very attracted to these substances.

- Human females also secrete aliphatic acids from the vaginal area.

Key Experiments in the Human Pheromone Story

- Berliner: The VNO and Pheromones

- The vomeronasal (VNO) organ responds to sex specific odors

Berliner's "Feel Good" Pheromone

- If it is a pheromone it must be sex specific

- If it is a pheromone it must be producing biological changes

- If it is a pheromone, it must be producing behavioral changes

Berliner's Famous Experiment

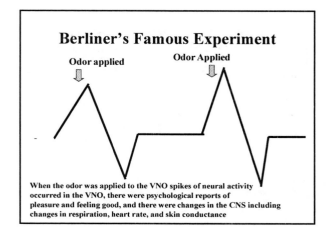

Odor applied   Odor Applied

When the odor was applied to the VNO spikes of neural activity occurred in the VNO, there were psychological reports of pleasure and feeling good, and there were changes in the CNS including changes in respiration, heart rate, and skin conductance

Pherin Pharmaceuticals Is Developing a Variety of Pheromonal Products to Treat Behavioral Conditions

- Products to alter
  - Mood
  - Sexual behavior
  - Body temperature
  - Appetite and sugar and fat metabolism
  - Water and electrolyte balance
  - Confidence

Major Findings of the McGill Sensory Deprivation Experiments

- Many of the volunteers (almost half) quit during the first 48 hours of the experiment

- Those who did stay showed considerable impairment in psychological functioning

  - Impaired problem solving ability
  - Impaired motor coordination
  - Organized thinking was compromised
  - Inability to concentrate
  - Inability to distinguish sleep from waking stages
  - Reports of high stress levels
  - Reports of being very frightened
  - 80% reported having some kind of hallucination

Three Stages of Memory

Retrieved

Sensory register
1. Large capacity
2. Contains sensory information
3. Very brief retention of images (up to 1/2 second for visual, 2 seconds for auditory)

Short-term memory (STM)
1. Limited capacity
2. Brief storage of items (up to 30 seconds if no rehearsal)
3. Involved in conscious processing of information

Long-term memory (LTM)
1. Unlimited capacity
2. Storage thought by some to be permanent
3. Information organized and indexed

Information from environment

Forgotten   Transferred   Forgotten   Transferred/Retrieved

Evidence for Separate Short and Long-term Memory Mechanisms

- Free recall studies

- Clinical observations

- Memory consolidation studies

The Serial Position Curve

List of words:

1. Tree
2. House
3. Rock
4. Car
5. Store
6. Road
7. Glass
8. Truck
9. Pencil
10. Lamp
11. Street
12. Light
13. Ball
14. Branch
15. Spoon

Words at the beginning of a list are remembered very well (lodged into long term memory – primacy effect), words at the end of a list are remembered very well (lodged into short term memory – recency effect), while words in the middle of a list are not remembered well.

Clinical Observations

- **Temporal lobe removal in severe epileptic patients**

  - Permanent loss of the ability to transfer new information from short to

---

Memory Consolidation Studies

- **Head Trauma Victims**

  - People involved in car accidents in which they receive a traumatic blow to the head suffer deficits in short term memory but not long term memory

---

Memory Consolidation Studies

- **Electroconvulsive shock therapy (ECT)**

  - Patients who receive ECS for depression frequently suffer deficits in short term memory but not long term memory

---

Memory Consolidation Studies

- **Laboratory studies with rats**

  - Rats that step down from a platform to a lower platform and then receive shock to their feet rarely step down again

  - Rats that receive ECS after stepping down on the lower platform, and then receive shock to their feet, fail to remember and step down on the lower platform on future occasions

---

The Search for the Engram

- The physical trace of memory

- Psychologists believe that every time we learn something, there is a resulting change in the biochemistry of the brain.

  - Is it electrical?
  - Is it change in morphology?
  - Is it change in protein synthesis?
  - Is it a change in neurotransmitters or hormones

Karl Lashley Searches for the Engram—The Physical Trace of Memory

•Cortical cuts had no effects on memory of a maze

•Tissue ablations had no effects on memory of a maze

•Lashley concluded that memory is stored throughout the central nervous system and there is not one specific brain area that is the locus for memory

Richard Thompson Locates the Brain Circuitry for Classical Conditioning of Rabbit Eye Blink Responses

Richard Thompson showed that the red nucleus of the cerebellum is important for the classically conditioned eyeblink response in the rabbit.

Thompson concluded that some simple memories have a very specific central nervous

Early Search for the Engram Biochemical/Neural Changes 1950-1960

- Halstead and Hayden
  - Learning by rats (rope climbing to receive a food reinforcement) is related to RNA and protein synthesis

Early Search for the Engram Biochemical/Neural Changes 1950-1960

- E Roy John

  - Breaking up memory for a visual discrimination in cats by ribonuclease injections

Early Search for the Engram Biochemical/Neural Changes 1950-1960

- Cameron

  - Injected drugs that boost RNA in senile people and improved memory

Early Search for the Engram Biochemical/Neural Changes 1950-1960

- Memory consolidation studies

  - Using ECS to slow down neural activity and impair memory

  - Using strychnine to speed up neural activity and improve memory in rats

James McConnell
Cannibalistic Transfer of Memory
1970-1980

- The unusual case of Planaria

- Where is the engram stored?

- Cannibalistic transfer

- Transfer of memory by RNA injections

Continuing the Engram Search
1980s and 1990s

- George Unger

  – habituation and memory transfer

  – Scotophobin and memory

Continuing the Engram Search
1980s and 1990s

- Jefferson
  – REM sleep and memory

  – Animals that exhibit more REM sleep on the night following learning a new task are better able to remember what they have learned

  – More new proteins are being produced during REM than at any other time in the sleep/wake cycle

Continuing the Engram Search
1980s and 1990s

- Agranoff

  – Broke up memory for an active avoidance response by injecting puromycin (which blocks proteins) in the brains of goldfish

Continuing the Engram Search
1980s and 1990s

- Lynch

  – Rats that learned a simple response showed increased dendritic sprouting in the hippocampus

Continuing the Engram Search:
Long Term Potentiation (LTP)

Neurobiologist Eric Kandel has shown that single neurons in the hippocampus become increasingly sensitive to stimulation and LTPs can continue for several weeks following their first stimulation.

State Dependent Memory

- Memory associated with a physiological state will be easier to retrieve when you are in the same physiological state

State Dependent Effects and Drugs

If drink during learning   *May recall better with drink*   *Than without*

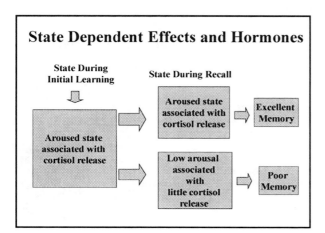

State Dependent Effects and Hormones

State During Initial Learning

State During Recall

Aroused state associated with cortisol release → Aroused state associated with cortisol release → Excellent Memory

Aroused state associated with cortisol release → Low arousal associated with little cortisol release → Poor Memory

Conclusion

- The biochemistry of learning and memory suggests that the formation of new proteins in the brain may produce morphological changes in discrete brain areas.

- These biochemical and morphological changes may be the keys to understanding how we learn, remember and forget.

Some Facts Regarding Laterality

- 93% of us are right handed; roughly 7% of us are left handed; only a small minority are ambidextrous

- If you are right handed, your <u>left hemisphere</u> is the dominant hemisphere

- If you are left handed, your <u>right hemisphere</u> is the dominant hemispher

Functions of the Two Hemispheres

- <u>Dominant hemisphere</u> is responsible for
  - Speech
  - Writing
  - Thinking

- <u>Minor hemisphere</u> is responsible for
  - Perceptual functions
  - Emotional functions
  - Monitoring functions

- How do we know that the two hemispheres serve different functions
  - Damage to the brain and <u>aphasia</u>

The Split Brain Procedure: Sperry and Myers

- In cats...corpus callosum is cut
  - Creation of two separate brains in the same animal

- In humans...corpus callosum is cut
  - Creation of two separate minds in the same body

The Basics of the EEG Machine

Scalp electrodes detect surface electrical brain wave activity from the cortex.

The EEG machine amplifies electrical brain waves from scalp electrodes.

Each electrode corresponds to an ink pen on the EEG machine.

The pen deflects when there is a current change and makes a mark on paper that is continuously advancing

Important Facts About Sleep

- We spend 30-40% of our live in sleep
- We (especially adolescents) don't get enough of it
- In some cultures, not having enough sleep is viewed as a badge of honor
- We are immobile and unconscious for 7-8 hours night at which time we are very vulnerable

Rats Kept Awake Indefinitely Starting Dying After 5 Days

Sleep is as essential as food and water for survival

One Night Without Sleep Disrupts Memory

- Subjects are 40% worse in memorizing lists of words

- One night of good sleep actually improves memory

- Practice.... with a night of sleep... makes perfect

What If You Sleep But Just Not Enough

- Chronic Partial Sleep Deprivation
  - Keep awake till 4 am..aroused at 8 am

- Results:
  - Impairment of attention
  - Impairment of memory
  - Impairment of speed of thinking
  - Impairment of alertness and reaction time
  - Each day, it accumulates

Dr David Dinges
University of Pennsylvania
Medical School

Micro-Sleeping

World Famous Accidents
Due to Sleep Impairment
- Exxon Valdez Oil Spill

World Famous Accidents
Due to Sleep Impairment
- Chernobyl

World Famous Accidents
Due to Sleep Impairment
- 3 Mile Island Disaster

World Famous Accidents
Due to Sleep Impairment

- Staten Island Ferry Crash

We are Getting
Less Sleep Than Ever

- 1960 Study: The average = 8 hours

- 2010 Study: The average = 6.7 hours

Less Sleep is Associated With Significant Health Problems

- Pre-diabetic state is produced in just 6 days following partial sleep deprivation

- Subjects were becoming hyperphagic
  - drop in leptin levels signaling the brain to eat

- More recent studies show an association with obesity, heart disease and stroke

Dr Eva Van Cauter
University of Chicago Medical School

Sleep Deprivation Disrupts Fruit Fly Sexual Behavior

Dr. Scott McRobert
St Joseph's University

Basics of Brain Wave Activity

- <u>Amplitude of a brain wave:</u>

  - How far does it deflect from its base

- <u>Frequency of a brain wave:</u>

  - How many deflections occur per unit o

Nathaniel Kleitman and William Dement Discover the Five Stages of Sleep

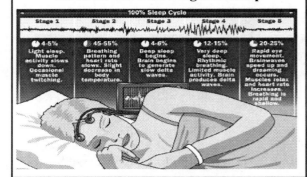

Characteristics of Rapid Eye Movement (REM) Sleep

- Sleep occurs in 90 minute cycles

- REM sleep is also called paradoxical sleep

- REM sleep is dominated by alpha like waves

- REM sleep is characterized by intense mental activity (dreaming)

- REM deprivation disrupts normal equilibrium

Psychology 101 – Part III

- Intelligence and Cognitive Processes

- Life Span Development

- Motivation

What is Intelligence?

- Intelligence is a very general mental capability that, among other things, involves the ability to:
  - Reason
  - Plan
  - Solve problems
  - Think abstractly
  - Comprehend complex ideas
  - Learn quickly
  - Learn from experience

Gardner's Eight Types of Intelligence

1. Logical-Mathematical Intelligence

- Sensitivity to, and capacity to discern, logical or numerical patterns; ability to handle long chains of reasoning

- Examples: Scientists, Mathematicians

Gardner's Eight Types of Intelligence

2. Linguistic Intelligence

- Sensitivity to the sounds, rhythms, and meaning of words; sensitivity to the different functions of language

- Examples: Poet, Journalist

Gardner's Eight Types of Intelligence

3. Naturalist Intelligence

- Sensitivity to the differences among diverse species; abilities to interact subtly with living creatures

- Examples: Biologist, Environmentalist

Gardner's Eight Types of Intelligence

4. Musical Intelligence

- Abilities to produce and appreciate rhythm, pitch, and timbre; appreciation of the forms of musical expressiveness

- Examples: Composers, Violinists

Gardner's Eight Types of Intelligence

5. Spatial Intelligence

- Capacities to perceive the visual-spatial world accurately and to perform transformations on one's initial perceptions

- Examples: Navigator, Sculptor

Gardner's Eight Types of Intelligence

6. Bodily Kinesthetic Intelligence

- Abilities to control one's body movement and to handle objects skillfully

- Examples: Dancer, Athlete

Gardner's Eight Types of Intelligence

7. Interpersonal Intelligence

- Capacities to discern and respond appropriately to the moods, temperaments, motivations, and desires of other people

- Examples: Therapist, Salesperson

Gardner's Eight Types of Intelligence

8. Intrapersonal Intelligence

- Access to one's own feelings and the ability to discriminate among them and draw upon them to guide behavior; knowledge of one's own strengths, weaknesses, desires, and intelligence

- Examples: Person with detailed, accurate self-knowledge

Sternberg's Triarchic Theory of Intelligence

- <u>Analytical</u>: involves the kinds of academically oriented problem-solving skills measured by traditional intelligence tests ("book smarts")

- <u>Practical</u>: refers to the skills need to cope with everyday demands and to manage oneself and other people effectively ("street smarts")

- <u>Creative</u>: comprises the mental skills needed to deal adaptively with novel problems ("divergent thinking")

Theory of Emotional Intelligence

- Ability to read others' emotions accurately

- Ability to respond to others' emotions accurately

- Ability to motivate oneself

- Ability to be aware of one's own emotions

- Ability to regulate and control one's own emotional responses

Alfred Binet and the First Intelligence Test

- In 1905, Alfred Binet created the first usable intelligence test in France

- Prior to Binet, intelligence was measured by:

  - Efficiency of eye-hand coordination
  - Ability to remember lists of nonsense syllables
  - Estimating the passage of time

Original Simon-Binet Test

- Test was originally devised by Binet and Simon to help those French school children who might need additional help
  - Modern versions of IQ tests have unfortunately become instruments of exclusion

- Binet gave the test to a large number of Paris school children and created a standard for each age group based on his data.
  - For example, if 70 percent of 8-year-olds could pass a particular test, then success on the test represented the 8-year-old level of intelligence

Examples from First Binet-Simon Test

- Three years
  - Shows nose eyes and mouth
  - Repeats two digits
  - Describes objects in a picture
  - Gives family name.
  - Repeats a sentence of six syllables.

- Six years
  - Distinguishes between morning and afternoon
  - Defines objects in terms of their use
  - Copies a shape.
  - Counts 13 pennies
  - Compares faces from the aesthetic point

  Test items were grouped on the basis of the age at which most children could complete them

Examples from First Binet-Simon Test

- Nine years
  - Defines objects in terms broader than their use
  - Recognizes all the pieces of our money
  - Names the months
  - Understands easy questions.

- Twelve years
  - Uses three given words in one sentence
  - Recalls more than 60 words in three minutes
  - Defines abstract terms
  - Understands a disarranged sentence.

  Test items were grouped on the basis of the age at which most children could complete them

Original Simon-Binet Test

- If a child of 11 years of age scored like an average 8 year old, the child was
  - considered to be 3 years retarded in mental development

- If a child of 9 years of age scored like an average 10 year old, the child was
  - considered to be 1 year advanced in mental development

William Stern and The Intelligence Quotient (IQ)

$$MA / CA \times 100 = IQ$$

Examples

$$10/10 \times 100 = 100$$

$$5/10 \times 100 = 50$$

$$10/5 \times 100 = 200$$

The Wechsler Tests

- Wechsler divided the concept of intelligence into two main areas:
  - verbal
  - performance (non-verbal)

- The Wechsler Adult Intelligence Scale (WAIS)

- Wechsler Intelligence Scale for Children (WISC)

- Presently the most commonly administered intelligence tests in the world

IQ is Normally Distributed

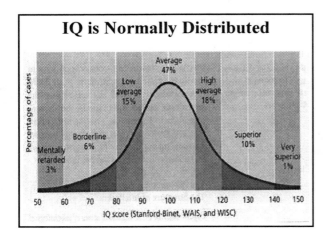

Two Extreme Views of Intelligence

- **Nature**: Our intelligence is a product of our genetic endowment

- **Nurture**: Our intelligence is a product of the environment and our experiences

The Correlation Coefficient

- No association   .00
- Low association   .25
- Moderate association   .50
- High association   .75
- Perfect association   1.00

What is the Correlation Between Your IQ and That of Your Biological Parents?

- The Correlation Coefficient is about:

».50

- Interpretation:

  - Similar genes....a genetic basis to intelligence

  - Environmental: Parents with high IQs are likely to create an intellectually stimulating environment for their kids

Understanding Twin Studies

- Identical twins Dan and Dave....100% sharing of genes
- If Dan has an IQ of 134, what is the likelihood that Dave also has an IQ of 134?
- Or, if Dan has an IQ of 84, what is the likelihood that Dave also has an IQ of 84?
- Is the degree of similarity in identical twins IQ greater than that seen in fraternal twins?

IQ and Heredity

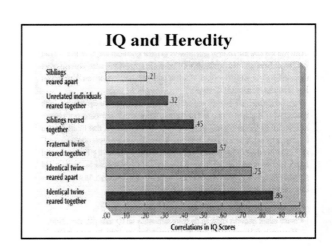

Harold Skeel's and the Iowa Orphanage Study

- Initial Observatons

- Skeels noticed two 3 year old girls in a state orphanage. They were:
  - Very sad and listless
  - Undersized for their age
  - Low IQs

- Some weeks later he observed the same two little girls and they were playing and running around like any other 3 year old toddlers

Harold Skeel's and the Iowa Orphanage Study

- The Experiment
- Skeels took other 3 year old orphans and brought them to another institution where they were reared with older retarded woman who could provide love, attention, and stimulation. They improved in:
  - Health
  - Happiness
  - Maturity
  - IQ ... increases ranged from 7 to 58 IQ points with an average increase of 28 points

- Orphans not reared by an older retarded woman showed losses in IQ ranging from 8 to 45 IQ points with average loss of 30 points

Harold Skeel's and the Iowa Orphanage Study

- Skeels studied the orphans for the next 30 years

  - As adults, children mothered by the older retarded woman were healthier, happier, better adjusted, and more productive than the controls

- Adoption studies show that placement in a good home increases IQ of adopted children beyond what would be predicted from the IQ of their biological parents.

The Divisive Research of Arthur Jensen

- In a 1969 article, Berkeley psychologist Arthur Jensen estimated that heredity accounts for about 80% of the individual differences in IQ

- African-Americans score on the average 10-15 points lower than Caucasians on standardized IQ tests

- Jensen concluded that there is an innate, genetically determined difference in IQ between African-Americans and Caucasians

Are Jensen's Conclusions Relevant?

- African-Americans and Caucasians show considerable individual variation in IQ and an individual score is not affected by the average of his or her race

- Any large difference in average inborn ability might greatly affect attempts to improve performance through changes in the educational system or establishment of programs such as Head Start

- Jensen's article, though it was considered opinion, has stirred up a great deal of emotion. It is approved by racists and deplored by enemies of racism.

Why Do African-Americans Score Lower Than Caucasians on IQ Tests?

- African-Americans as well as Caucasians from rural backgrounds and low socioeconomic conditions score lower on standard intelligence tests because they have not had equal exposure to the kind of white middle class culture upon which intelligence tests are based

An Important Study to Remember

- 130 black and interracial children were adopted into white families that were above average in education, occupational status

- The adopted children were found to have an average IQ of 106, which is higher than the national average of 100.

Shattering Some Myths About Racial Differences in IQ

- Although African-Americans and Caucasians may differ in physical appearance, they do not represent distinct biological groups.

- Differences in gene structures, where they are known, are greater within races than between them!!!!!

An Important Study to Remember Concerning Race and IQ

- Among black populations, there is some tendency for lightness of skin color (which presumably is an indication of the degree of intermixture with whites) to correlate positively with IQ.

- Importantly, such correlations are very low (.15) and can be explained on the basis of environmental differences

  - Lighter skin color is associated with less discrimination and greater opportunity

  - A recent study showed no relationship between degree of African ancestry and intellectual ability.

An Important Study to Remember Concerning Race and IQ

- A study of illegitimate children fathered by US serviceman during the post WW II occupation of Germany found no IQ differences between children whose fathers were black and those whose fathers were white.

- The children were raised by white German mothers of similar social status and were matched with children of the same age in the classroom

Reaction Range Concept
Phenotype

High   Low

Environment

High   Low

Genotype for Trait

Definition for Development

All the processes of change through which a person's potential behaviors evolve.

These developmental changes may emerge as new qualities, abilities or traits

Qualitative and Quantitative Changes in Behavior

- <u>Qualitative</u> (developmental) changes that are related to experience and learning.

  - For example, changes in social behavior as you mature.

- <u>Quantitative</u> (maturational) changes are predisposed by heredity and allowed by the environment. They are related to physical growth.

  - For example, learning to ride a bicycle or water ski.

Piaget and Freud: Two Examples of Stage Theorists

- Intellectual and emotional development passes through distinct <u>stages</u>

- The <u>speed</u> through the stages can vary dramatically from individual to individual

- The <u>order</u> that a child goes through these stages is the same from individual to individual

Piaget's Theory Important Concepts

- <u>Intelligence</u>: The ability to adapt to , and cope with the environment the individual lives in

- <u>Assimilation</u>: Taking in information about the world, digesting it, making it similar to us or rearranging it so that it suits our needs

- <u>Accommodation</u>: An intellectual adjustment made to take in information

Piaget's Stages of Cognitive Development Stage 1: Sensorimotor Period

<u>Age</u>	<u>Accomplishment</u>	<u>Major Outcome</u>
Birth to 2 years of age	Infants learn to integrate input and motor output and begin to use symbolic thought	Object permanence

Piaget's Stages of Cognitive Development Stage 2: Preoperational Period

<u>Age</u>	<u>Accomplishment</u>	<u>Major Outcome</u>
2 to 7	Children become more sophisticated in their use of language and symbolic thought but they have difficulty in reasoning logically	Loss of egocentrism

Piaget's Stages of Cognitive Development Stage 3: Concrete Operations

<u>Age</u>	<u>Accomplishment</u>	<u>Major Outcome</u>
7-11	Children become proficient in reasoning logically about concrete situations such as the ability to make transitive inferences	Conservation

Piaget's Stages of Cognitive Development
Stage 4: Formal operations

Age	Accomplishment	Major Outcome
11-15	Many adolescents learn to use abstract reasoning and to form hypotheses about future events based on relevant current knowledge	Abstract reasoning and hypothesis testing

Freud's Stages of Psychosexual Development

- Oral (0-18 months)

- Erogenous Zone
  – The mouth

- Key conflict or developmental task
  – weaning from the breast or bottle

Freud's Stages of Psychosexual Development

- Anal (18 months to 3 years)

- Erogenous Zone
  – The anus

- Key conflict or developmental task
  – Toilet training

Freud's Stages of Psychosexual Development

- Phallic (3 to 6 years)

- Erogenous Zone
  – The genitals

- Key conflict or developmental task
  – Overcoming the Oedipus complex by identifying with same sex parents

Freud's Stages of Psychosexual Development

- Latency (6 years to puberty)

- Erogenous Zone
  – None

- Key conflict or developmental task
  – Interacting with same sex peers

Freud's Stages of Psychosexual Development

- Genital (puberty to adult life)

- Erogenous Zone
  – The genitals

- Key conflict or developmental task
  – Establishing intimate relationships with members of the opposite sex

Harry Harlow
A Pioneering Psychologist

- Was first interested in studying the effects of brain lesions on learning and memory

- Decided to establish a breeding colony of chimpanzees at Wisconsin to reduce his animal costs

- Separated infants from their mothers to reduce transfer of contagious diseases

- Raised infants in isolation with a baby blanket

- Infants showed profound distress when blanket was removed

Harlow's Five Types of Love

- The love an infant shows for its mother

- The love for others one's own age (peer love)

- The love for members of the opposite sex (heterosexual love)

- The love a mother shows for its infants (motherly love)

- The love a father shows for its infants

Harlow's Essential Ingredients for Love and Attachment

- <u>Warmth</u>: For the first two weeks of life this is the critical stimulus

- <u>Contact comfort</u>: After the first two weeks of life, close contact between the infant and the mother's abdomen is critical for attachment

- <u>Trust</u>: The bond between a mother and its infant is solidified when the infant comes to know that its mother will be there for comfort and defense

Harlow's Monster Mothers

- Air blast mother

- Violent shaking mother

- Catapult mother

- Spike mother

- Cold mother

Effects of Prolonged Social Deprivation

- Harlow showed that prolonged social deprivation (isolation from peers) produced a number of effects:

  - Reduced sexual behavior

  - Reduced aggression

  - Severe depression-like symptoms comparable to <u>anacilitic</u> depression seen in humans

What Kind of Mothers are Animals that were Socially Deprived?

- Once socially deprived females became pregnant and gave birth to their own offspring, many of them became "monster" mothers killing and eating (infanticide) their own offspring

- On future pregnancies, many of the females reverted back to being maternal

Harlow's Early Social Deprivation Research: Implications for Humans

- Increasingly researchers are finding that parents of abused children were socially isolated during their early upbringing.

- This suggests that isolation/social deprivation may be a key ingredient to understanding instances of human child abuse

Motivation Model

S – O – R

The attempt to explain internal processes that come between independent variables and dependent variables

Single Most Important Concepts in Studying Motivation

- We can ascribe motivation to people only when we can infer that their behaviors are intentional

- Some aspects of motivation may be deeply buried in the unconscious

Important Concepts for Understanding the Area of Motivation

- <u>Motives</u> are anything that initiate behavior

- <u>Drives</u> are urges to engage in action
  - Primary drives (e.g, hunger)
  - Learned drives (e.g, desire or approval

- <u>Incentives</u> are objects or conditions in the environment that stimulate behavior

The Difference Between Primary and Learned Drives

- <u>Primary Drives</u> keep us alive and healthy by satisfying our basic body needs

- <u>Learned Drives</u> primarily help us to adjust to our social environment

Major Defining Characteristics of Motivated Behavior

- <u>Arousal</u>: A motive makes us feel more active and restless

- <u>Direction</u>: Motivated behavior has purpose, intention, aim, a goal

- <u>Desire</u>: Experienced as tension, strain, and expectation

The Primary Theories of Motivated Behavior

- The Pleasure-Pain Theory (Hedonism)

- The Reflex-Drive Theory

- The Instinct Theory

The Pleasure Pain Theory of Motivation

- We seek pleasurable situations in our lives and avoid painful ones.

- <u>Problems with the theory:</u> Sometimes we actually seek out painful situations.

The Reflex-Drive Theory of Motivated Behavior

- <u>Reflex Component:</u> Our behavior is nothing more than an automatic response to a stimulus

- <u>Problems:</u> Correct stimulus present but no response

- <u>Drive Component:</u> Our behavior is stimulated by internal drive stimuli

- <u>Problems:</u> Our behavior can persist without an internal drive stimulus

Instinct Theory of Motivated Behavior

- <u>Instinct:</u> An inborn predisposition to act in a particular way.

- Many scientists believe that mating behavior, aggression, and maternal behavior are instinctive

- Konrad Lorenz and Niko Tinbergen, European ethologists and Nobel Prize winners, revived instinct theory and started looking at <u>species specific behaviors</u> and the <u>adaptive significance of behavior</u>

Instinct Theory of Motivated Behavior

- Lorenz and Tinbergen looked at <u>fixed action patterns</u> that are set in motion by <u>releasor stimuli</u>

- Young herring gulls peck the red spot on their mother's beak which causes her to regurgitate food and deliver it to them

- <u>Problems:</u> Instinct theory, while appropriate for lower animals, simply can't account for the many complex behaviors seen in humans

Schacter's Experiment on Time Perception in Obese and Normal Subjects

- Hypothesis

  - Normal subjects will eat when their bodies tell them to (i.e., they will respond to internal controls

  - Obese subjects will eat "by the clock" regardless of what their stomachs and feeding centers say

Stanley Schacter's Research Comparing Obese and Normal Subjects

	Before Dinner*	After Dinner*
NORMAL	Average	Average
OBESE	Very Few	Many

* Crackers Eaten

Other Characteristics of Obese and Normal Subjects

- Obese subjects are plate cleaners
  - Large portions
  - Small portions

- Obese subjects are affected by the taste of food

- Obese subjects are less likely to perform physical labor for food or suffer mild amounts of pain to get food

What are the Signals for Hunger?

- Empty stomach?

- External stimuli?

- Habits and customs?

Anorexia Nervosa

- Afflicts woman (15 to 24 years of age) more than men (10 to 1)

- Intense fear of eating

- Distortion of body image

- Unrelenting pursuit of thinness

- Exercise obsessed

- Can cause fatal damage to heart muscle

- Perfectionist personalities

Anorexia Nervosa in the Fiji Islands

- Prior to the 1990s, the incidence of anorexia nervosa in the Fiji islands was near zero

- Once American television programming like *90210* and *Melrose Place* became available by Satelite, the incidence of anorexia nervosa dramatically increased

Initial Clinical Observations

- Patients with tumors or damage to the hypothalamus frequently became hyperphagic (overate) and became obese.

- This suggested animal experimentation to locate precisely the areas of the brain involved in feeding and hunger

The Hypothalamic Circuitry for Feeding

- **Lateral hypothalamus (LH):**

  – initiates eating behavior; it is our feeding center

- **Ventromedial hypothalamus (VMH or VMN):**

  – inhibits eating; it is our satiety center

Stimulation and Lesion Studies by Epstein

- **Stimulate the LH:** A satiated animal will quickly begin to eat

- **Stimulate the VMN:** A food deprived animal will quickly stop eating

- **Lesion the LH:** An animal will become aphagic and adipsic and must be force fed

- **Lesion the VMN:** An animal will become hyperphagic and obese

Characteristics of the Obese VMN Lesion Animal

- They overeat only if the food is palatable

- They overeat only if the texture of the food is just right

- They overeat only if the temperature of the food is just right

- They won't work very hard to obtain food

- They won't tolerate pain to obtain food

Two Hypothalamic Feeding Systems

- **Short-term system:**

  – Tells when to start and stop a meal

- **Long-term system:**

  – Tells us to maintain a stable body we

Short Term Factors: Blood Sugar Levels

- Low blood sugar makes you feel weak and hungry
  - **Inject insulin:** blood sugar decreases and it increases food intake
  - **Inject glucose:** blood sugar increases and food intake decreases

- Glucoreceptors in the hypothalamus are sensitive to the rate of flow of glucose through cells

- Neural activity in the hypothalamus changes as a function of high or low glucose

Short Term Factors: Stomach Fullness

- **Full stomach:** VMN neurons are activated and food intake is decreased

- **Empty stomach:** LH neurons are activated and food intake is increased

Short Term Factors: Body Temperature

- Thermosensitive neurons in the hypothalamus

  - When the hypothalamus is heated, food intake is decreased

  - When the hypothalamus is cooled, food intake is increased

Summary of LH and VMH Involvement in Food Intake

- Lateral hypothalamus (LH) responds to:
  - Low blood sugar
  - Increase stomach contractions
  - Low brain temperature

- Ventromedial hypothalamus (VMH) responds to:
  - High blood sugar
  - Stomach tension
  - High brain temperature

Long-term Control of Food Intake: Central Factors

- <u>Damage to the VMN</u>
  - Overeating following restriction
  - Long term brain set point has been set higher

- <u>Damage to the LH</u>
  - Refusal to eat and must be force fed
  - Long term brain set point has been set lower

Long-term Control of Food Intake: Peripheral Factors

- Adipose cells can expand in size dramatically
  - Physical difference in size between normal and obese subjects is related to this

- Fat is stored in adipose tissue and is responsible in part for long term control of food intake

- When you are in a period of fasting, fat cells release fatty acids and glycerol

- Glycerol is converted to glucose

Long-term Control of Food Intake: Appetite Hormones

- <u>Insulin</u>: hormone secreted by pancreas controls blood glucose

- <u>Leptin</u>: protein secreted by fat cells; when abundant, causes brain to increase metabolism and decrease hunger

- <u>Orexin</u>: hunger triggering hormone secreted by the hypothalamus

- <u>Ghrelin</u>: hormone secreted by empty stomach; sends "I'm hungry" signals to the brain

- <u>PYY</u>: Digestive tract hormone, sends "I'm not hungry" signals to the brain

Major Characteristics of Aggressive Behavior

- Overt behavior involving intent to inflict noxious stimulation or to behave destructively toward another organism.

- Aggressive behavior can be direct or indirect

- Under conditions of aversive stimulation or frustration, aggressive destructive behavior may be directed toward inanimate objects

- The important factor is the <u>intent or perceived intent</u> of the behaving individual

The Major Determinants of Aggressive Behavior

- Environmental factors

- Instinctive factors

- Biological factors

The Case for Environmental Factors

- Could it be that societal factors, like differences in handgun ownership, drastically alter our outlook on aggressive and violent behaviors?

  - Detroit, Michigan: 2 million people and about 700 gun related homicides each year

  - England: 50 million people and only 150 gun related homicides each year.

Aggression: Nature or Nurture?

Nature or Nurture? From a very early age, Andrew Golden was taught to fire hunting rifles. At the age of 11, he and his friend, Mitchell Johnson, killed four classmates and a teacher at an elementary school in Jonesboro, Arkansas. Was this tragedy the result of nature or nurture?

The Case for Environmental Factors

- Viewing television violence

  - 82% of all primetime entertainment shows contain violence

  - The more violence and aggression a youngster watches on TV, regardless of their age, sex, or social background, the more aggressive they are likely to be in their attitudes and behavior

  - Parents who watched more TV as children tended to punish their own children more severely

  - The famous NOTEL study in Canada

The Case for Environmental Factors

- Is the viewing of pornography responsible for violence toward woman?

  - Yes: Of women who reported abuse by their partner, a high percentage of their partners (41%) used pornographic material

  - Yes: Prolonged exposure to pornography leads to greater acceptance of rape and abuse of woman

  - No: Male dominance and power structure in our society, not pornography, causes violence toward women

Konrad Lorenz: Aggressive Instinct in Male Stickleback Fish

- Animals of one species will often kill members of another species for food or if threatened but they seldom kill out of hatred, prejudice or for the fun of it....these are distinctly human traits

- Instinctive aggression in male stickleback fish: the head dipping response

  - All males exhibit the response even if isolated from an early age

  - The response is very stereotyped and is the same in all males

  - The behavior intensifies in males during the

Nathan Azrin's Major Findings on Shock-Induced Aggression

- The stronger the shock, the longer the aggression lasts

- The more frequent the shock, the more vigorous and vicious the attacks

- Animals don't habituate

- Isolation from the time of birth does not diminish the response

- Females are as likely as males to fight

- Psychologically painful stimuli (frustration) can also cause aggression

The Dollard-Miller Frustration Aggression Hypothesis

- Frustration occurs whenever a highly motivated organism encounters a barrier that prevents him from reaching a goal.

- The barrier can be physical, psychological, or symbolic.

- If an organism can't get around the barrier, their behavior becomes frustrated, less logical, and more emotional

The Kleuver-Bucy Syndrome

- Highly aggressive male Rhesus monkeys had portions of their amygdala surgically removed

- After the surgery the males become docile and calm

- They would rarely show aggression even when attacked by another male

Flynn's Research on Predatory and Irritable Aggression in Cats

- Stimulation of the lateral hypothalamus (LH) produced predatory aggression and "quiet biting attack". The cat would suddenly pounce on the rat and deliver fatal biting blows to the head and neck

- Stimulation of the medial hypothalamus (MH) produced "irritable aggression". The cat would arch its back, hiss, snarl, bare its teeth and eventually attack and bite the rat

Testosterone and Aggression

- What are hormones?
  - Chemicals secreted by endocrine glands which are known to have distinct effects on the morphology and behavior of individuals

- The testes: Male reproductive glands that secrete testosterone

- The ovaries: Female reproductive glands that secrete estrogen and progesterone

- Sex differences in the aggressive behavior of humans and lower animals

Edwards Important Studies on Testosterone and Aggression

- Male mice were castrated at the time of birth and then tested for aggression as adults.

  - Few of the animals exhibited aggression

- Female mice were given a single injection of testosterone on the day of birth and then were tested for aggression.

  - They behaved like normal males and exhibited high levels of aggression

Human Research on Clinical Syndromes

- Money and Ehrhardt's research on elevated masculine behaviors accompanying Progestin-Induced Hermaphroditism (PIH) in genetic females

- Reinish's work on prenatal progestin exposure and aggressive attitude and behavior in genetic females

Human Research on Clinical Syndromes

- Progestin-Induced Hermaphroditism (PIH) accidentally produced in genetic females whose mothers were prescribed progestins because of at risk pregnancy conditions

- It resulted in females that acted like tomboys
  - Elevated levels of rough and tumble play
  - Elevated energy expenditure
  - Preferences for masculine clothing
  - Indifferent to babies
  - Preference for non domestic career
  - Lagged behind agemates in dating interest

- Caution: Biological or environmental?

Human Research on Clinical Syndromes

- Reinish's work on prenatal progestin exposure and aggressive attitude and behavior

- The study was better controlled
  - Age matched controls
  - Progestin exposure was limited the last trimester of pregnancy
  - More accurate tests of personality and aggressive attitudes

- Genetic females exposed to prenatal progestins were much more masculine in their behaviors and personalities

Sexual Motivation

- Every year many men and woman will seek help from their physicians in understanding their sexual motivation and that of their partner

- Physicians and psychiatrists are often times ill equipped at giving good advice

- In spite of its obvious importance to species survival, sexual motivation is still not understood as well as other aspects of motivation

Some Historical Moments in the History of Sex Research

- John Watson's unethical sex research

  - Recording of EEG activity

Some Historical Moments in the History of Sex Research

- Sigmund Freud and the concept of libido

  - The sexual nature of the libido is the driving force in behavior

The Major Findings from Alfred Kinsey's Famous Sex Survey

Males reporting anal sex with spouse: 11 percent.

Nearly 46 percent of males had bisexual experiences.

Between 6 and 14 percent of females had bisexual experiences.

Whereas nearly 21 percent of the males had experienced intercourse at age 16, only 6 percent of females had done so.

Males reporting premarital sex: 67 to 98 percent (varied by economic level).

Females reporting premarital sex: 50 percent.

Nearly 50 percent of all married males had some extramarital experiences, whereas 26 percent of married females had extramarital experiences.

About 10 percent of males were predominantly homosexual.

Between 2 and 6 percent of females were predominantly homosexual.

Males who reported masturbating: 92 percent.

Females who reported masturbating: 62 percent.

Master's and Johnson Research and Sex Therapy

- Males and females go through the same sexual response cycle: excitement, plateau, orgasm, resolution

- Sexual problems such as premature ejaculation and frigidity are not caused by repression and guilt (Freudian concepts)

- Problems in sexual function often are due to ignorance and the failure to learn adequate sexual responses…the failure to learn arousal signals from a partner

- The new sex therapy involves the use of sexual surrogates

Organization-Activation Theory of Testosterone Effects on Behavior

Organization	Activation
Prenatal/Early Neonatal T	Pubertal and Adult T

- Testosterone during early life has a dual action: 1) It masculinizes the brain (promotes male characterizes) and 2) it defeminizes the brain (suppresses female characteristics)

- Testosterone during pubertal and adult life activates behavior

Hormones and Male Sexual Behavior in Lower Animals

- Sexual activity in the male is acyclic
- Puberty and the onset of sexual activity
- Castration and replacement therapy with T
- Implants of T in the hypothalamus
- Presence of T early in life is essential

Hormones and Female Sexual Behavior in Lower Animals

- Sexual behavior in the female is cyclic

- Ovariectomy eliminates sexual behavior while estrogen and progesterone restores it

- Implants of estrogen and progesterone in the hypothalamus activate sexual behavior

- The absence of testosterone early in life is a requirement for female sexual behavior

Hormones and Sexual Behavior

- Methodological problems

  - Tremendous complexity of psychological, social, and cultural factors
  - Lack of scientifically valid experimentation

- We are forced to rely on information from clinical reports of patients suffering from clinical and/or mental disorders

  - Lack of good control procedures
  - Questionable validity of patient-doctor interviews

Hormones and Sexual Behavior in the Human Female

- No significant changes in female sexual behavior following premenopausal ovariectomy or menopause

- Involvement of adrenal testosterone?

- Evidence that hormones modulate sexual arousal in the human female

Hormones and Sexual Behavior in the Human Male

- Variable effects of castration in the human

- Hypogonadism reduces sexual interest

- Treatment of hypogonadal males with testosterone elevates sexual interest

Is Sexual Orientation in Males Related to Testosterone?

- Studies examining pubertal testosterone levels and male sexual orientation show no relationship

- Studies examining adult testosterone levels and male sexuality show no relationship

- Does not rule out the possibility that abnormal testosterone exposure during early (prenatal) life might influence sexual orientation in males

Prenatal Stress Elevates Male Homosexuality

- Dr. Gunter Dorner examined the incidence of male homosexuality in the male offspring of woman who were in the last trimester of pregnancy during the WW II bombing of Berlin.

- His results showed a higher than normal incidence of male homosexuality in their offspring

Prenatal Stress in Male Rats Elevates Female Sexual Behavior and Reduces Male Sexual Behavior

- Ward stressed pregnant female rats during the last trimester of pregnancy

- The male offspring, when allowed to grow to adulthood
  - showed elevated levels of female sexual behavior when given estrogen and progesterone
  - Showed reduced levels of male sexual behavior

- Fetal male rats whose mothers are stressed show reduced levels of testosterone during prenatal life

Simon Levay's Research on Heterosexual and Homosexual Brains

Levay took a look at the brains of heterosexual males and females and homosexual males.

<u>Major Finding</u>: One part of the hypothalamus is larger in the brains of heterosexual men than homosexual men or heterosexual women

<u>Complicating factor</u>: Many of the homosexual males were suffering from AIDS and the impact of this on the brain is unknown

Sexual Orientation: Female Lesbianism

- Money and Ehrhardt: Adrenogenital syndrome and elevated lesbianism

- Bailly and Pillard: For lesbians and homosexuals, concordance rates are higher in identical twins than fraternal twins

- The famous case of John/Joan: Identical twin males in which one was raised as male and the other female. The female ultimately reverted to male

The Famous Case of John/Joan

John/Joan at an early age (pictures 1 and 2) and during late adolescence (picture 3)

Conclusion

- The case of John/Joan suggests that the organ that determines the course of psychosocial development is the brain.

- It also indicates that sexual identity is a product of testosterone effects on the brain during prenatal life.

- If sexual orientation is about nature, then social policy needs to change in how we treat gays and lesbians.

Psychology 101 – Part IV

- **Personality**

- **Nature and Causes of Mental Disorder**

- **Treatment of Mental Disorders**

- **Social Psychology, Society, Culture**

The Four Major Approaches to the Study of Personality

- **Energy System Approach**

- **The Behavioral System Approach**

- **The Self Actualization Approach**

- **The Social System Approach**

Psychoanalytic Theory

- Freud's attempt to solve <u>hysteria</u>

- Why do patients suddenly become blind or become paralyzed even though there is no physical (organic) basis for it?

- Why does recovery occur following recall of an early traumatic experience either through hypnosis or free recall?

Psychoanalytic Theory

- **Energy concepts**
  - **Sexual instinct (libido)**
  - **Aggressive (death) instinct**

- **Discharge of energy**
  - **Libidinal discharge**
  - **Aggressive discharge**

- **Psychopathology results when the discharge of energy is blocked**

Ego Defense Mechanisms

- The ego defends itself against conflicts and anxieties by relegating unpleasant thoughts and impulses to the unconscious

Ego Defense Mechanisms

- **Repression**

  - **Rejecting unacceptable thoughts and banishing them to the unconscious**

  - **Example:** Repressing unacceptable sexual and aggressive impulses

Ego Defense Mechanisms

- **Rationalization**

  - **Proving that your actions are justifiable**

  - **Example:** Missing a deadline for a job

Ego Defense Mechanisms

- **Projection**

  - **Attributing a repressed desire to someone else**

  - **Example:** A woman growing tired of her lover

Ego Defense Mechanisms

- **Reaction Formation**

  - **Transforming the expression of a repressed motive into its opposite**

  - **Example:** hostility is replaced by friend

Ego Defense Mechanisms

- <u>Sublimation</u>

  - Transforming sexual and aggressive energy into acceptable motives

  - <u>Example</u>: Channeling libidinal drives into creative endeavors

Ego Defense Mechanisms

- <u>Displacement</u>

  - Diverting a behavior away from its natural target toward a less threatening target

  - <u>Example</u>: A person angry with their boss yells at their best friend

Ego Defense Mechanisms

- <u>Denial</u>

  - The refusal to believe information that provokes anxiety

  - <u>Example</u>: An alcoholic insisting that they do not have problem

Ego Defense Mechanisms

- <u>Regression</u>

  - Returning to a more immature level of functioning to avoid anxiety

  - <u>Example</u>: A young adult going through a divorce and becoming dependent upon his/her parents

Analytic Theory

- Carl Jung breaks with Freud

- Functions of the libido are broadened

- Personal unconscious

- Collective unconscious

- Archetypes (*animus* and *anima*)

- Extroversion and introversion

Behavioral System Approach

- Focus on <u>observable behaviors</u> of individuals rather than on internal hypothetical entities

- Trait Theories
  - descriptive analysis of behavior

- Learning Theories
  - how behavior is acquired and maintained

Trait Theory

- **How trait theories are developed**
  - Start with a simple observation
    - Joe behaved generously when asked to donate some of his time to a local charity
    - Joe is a generous person
  - A trait is born when we compare Joe with others in terms of generosity

- **Implicit in the process:**
  - Characteristic behaviors reflect predispositions to behave in particular ways
  - Predispositions are stable and consistent from one situation to another

- **Traits are the basic units of personality**

Trait Theory

- **Allport's trait theory**
  - Common traits
  - Individual traits
  - Cardinal traits
  - Central traits
  - Secondary traits

- **Criticism of trait theory**
  - Traits are treated as causes of behavior without giving sufficient weight to the role of external environment

Learning Theory

- **Bandura's Theory of Observational Learning**
  - Our personalities develop from what we see others do and whether or not they are punished or reinforced for their behavior

- **Bandura's famous Bobo Doll experiment**
  - Young kids watched other kids hitting a plastic doll. When they had a chance to interact with the doll their behavior was consistent with what they saw and whether or not there was punishment or praise for behavior

Rotter's Concept of Locus of Control

- **The learning of expectations**

- **Internal locus of control**
  - I am the master of my own ship

- **External locus of control**
  - I have no control over the events in my life. They are determined by fate and chance

Maslow and Self Actualization The Hierarchy of Needs

- **Basic needs (deficiency needs):** hunger, thirst, sex, security

- **Meta needs (growth needs):** spiritual/metaphysical

- **Peak experiences:** The time at which self actualization occurs

Harry Stack Sullivan's Social System Approach

- **Norms**
  - Rules of behavior accepted by group members

- **Roles**
  - Consistent patterns of individual behavior which are governed by norms associated with the group

- **Role Strain**
  - Being unable to perform a particular role satisfactorily

Harry Stack Sullivan's Social System Approach

- **Psychoanalytic theory does not recognize the importance of social relationship and the need for**
  - Acceptance
  - Respect
  - Love
- **A person needs to feel secure in how they are treated by others**
- **Mental illness results from insecurities**

Harry Stack Sullivan's Social System Approach

- The Self-System is derived from conceptions of ourselves and others

  - "good-me" acceptance by others

  - "bad-me" tensions and anxieties of others

  - "not-me" the dissociated self...being unacceptable to yourself and others

Some Facts Regarding Testing

- Poor Americans and black Americans score lower on standard intelligence tests that rich Americans and white Americans

- Large corporations have designed personality tests and aptitude tests that allow them to determine which job applicants are likely to do well and which are not.

- Psychotics score differently from normal persons on many personality tests

Core Concepts in Testing

- **Reliability:** Consistency or stability of scores on a test

- **Validity:** How well does a test measure what it says it is measuring

- **Norms:** Comparing an individual score to a standardization group

The Concept of Reliability

- **Test-retest reliability:** Are scores on the test stable over time?

- **Internal reliability:** Do all the items on the test measure the same thing as indicated by high correlations among them

- **Interjudge reliability:** Do different raters or scorers agree on their scoring or observations

Methods of Insuring Reliability

- Having two different people scoring the test independently from each other

- Administering a test at two different times (test-retest)

The Concept of Reliability

- **Test-retest reliability**

<u>**S-B IQ**</u>
<u>**Test Jan, 2003**</u>

<u>**S-B IQ**</u>
<u>**Test, Jan, 2004**</u>

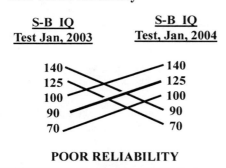

140
125
100
90
70

140
125
100
90
70

POOR RELIABILITY

The Concept of Reliability

- **Test-retest reliability**

<u>**S-B IQ**</u>
<u>**Test Jan, 2003**</u>

<u>**S-B IQ**</u>
<u>**Test, Jan, 2004**</u>

140 ——————— 140
125 ——————— 125
100 ——————— 100
90 ——————— 90
70 ——————— 70

VERY GOOD RELIABILITY

The Concept of Validity

- <u>Concurrent Validity</u>: To what extent is the test actually measuring the construct of interest (e.g., intelligence)?

- <u>Predictive Validity</u>: Do scores on the test predict some present or future behavior or outcome assumed to be affected by the construct being measured?

- <u>Content Validity</u>: Do the questions or test items relate to all aspects of the construct being measured?

The Concept of Validity

- **Concurrent Validity**

<u>**MMPI**</u>

<u>**PI**</u>

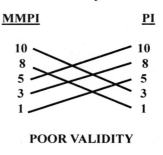

10
8
5
3
1

10
8
5
3
1

POOR VALIDITY

The Concept of Validity

- **Concurrent Validity**

<u>**MMPI**</u>

<u>**CPI**</u>

10 ——————— 10
8 ——————— 8
5 ——————— 5
3 ——————— 3
1 ——————— 1

GOOD VALIDITY

Personality Inventories

- Carefully standardized tests that contain a number of scales, each measuring a different personality dimension

- When a person takes a personality inventory, he/she responds to a series of personal statements

- A single personality inventory yields scores on a number of scales

The Minnesota Multiphasic Personality Inventory (MMPI)

- Originally devised to provide a quick assessment of mental disorder

- 14 scales, 10 of which are designed to examine the degree to which a person suffers from a particular mental disorder

Development of an MMPI Scale

- Depression scale: DSM defines "pure" depression as intense unhappiness, poor morale, lack of hope about the future. This is the criterion group

- 500 test questions are administered to the criterion group and a group of normal subjects

- The test questions in which the 2 groups differ reliably become the items for the depression scale

Sample Question on the MMPI Depression Scale

- The question below was selected for the MMPI depression scale. Depressed subjects almost always respond "yes" while normal subjects almost always respond "no".

- *I am frequently unhappy throughout the day and do not wish to have any human contacts.*

MMPI Scales

- Hypochondriasis

- Description:
  - Excessive concern about self and physical health, fatigue, a pattern of complaining

- Sample test item:
  - *I have a great deal of stomach trouble*

MMPI Scales

- Hysteria

- Description:
  - Use of physical symptoms to gain attention from others or avoid social responsibility

- Sample test item:
  - *I have had fainting spells*

MMPI Scales

- Psychopathic deviation

- Description:
  - Disregard for social rules and authority, impulsive, unreliable, self-centered, has shallow relationships

- Sample test item:
  - *In school I was sometimes sent to the principal for cutting up"*

MMPI Scales

- **Masculinity/Femininity**

- Description:
    - Identification with masculine and/or feminine sex roles

- Sample test item:
    - *I enjoy reading love stories*

MMPI Scales

- Paranoia

- Description:
    - Feelings of persecution and/or grandeur, suspiciousness, hypersensitivity, use of blame and projection

- Sample test item:
    - *I am sure I get a raw deal from life*

MMPI Scales

- Psychasthenia

- Description:
    - Anxiousness as exhibited in fears, self-doubt, worries, guilt, obsessions and compulsions

- Sample test item:
    - *I feel anxiety about something or someone almost all the time*

MMPI Scales

- Schizophrenia

- Description:
    - Feelings of social alienation, aloofness, confusion and disorientation, bizarre thoughts and sensations

- Sample test item:
    - *I often feel as though things were not real*

MMPI Scales

- Mania

- Description:
    - Hyperactivity, excitement, elation, euphoria, and excessive optimism

- Sample test item:
    - *At times my thoughts race ahead faster than I could speak them*

MMPI Scales

- Social introversion

- Description:
    - Withdrawal from social contact, isolation, shyness, a reserved, inhibited, self-effacing style

- Sample test item:
    - *Whenever possible I avoid being in*

Projective Test Characteristics

- Subjects are asked to respond in any way they desire to unstructured or ambiguous stimuli

- Because the stimuli are vague, people project their own personal characteristics into their responses

Sentence Completion Test

- The happiest time _____
- My mother _____
- My greatest fear _____
- The future _____
- My father _____
- My mind _____
- People _____

Sentence Completion Test: Sample Answers

- **The happiest time** *is when I am doing something well.*
- **My mother** *has always encouraged me.*
- **My greatest fear** *is that I will fail.*
- **The future** *is a challenge.*
- **My father** *is a successful man.*
- **My mind** *is clear and strong.*
- **People** *are fun to be with.*

A well adjusted person

Sentence Completion Test: Sample Answers

- **The happiest time** *is now.*
- **My mother** *is a woman..*
- **My greatest fear** *is yet to come.*
- **The future** *is tomorrow.*
- **My father** *is a businessman.*
- **My mind** *is my brain.*
- **People** *come in all shapes and sizes.*

A person who is very literal minded and very guarded

Interpreting the Rorshach Inkblot Test

- Initially developed by Herman Rorshach to examine fantasy and perception, now used for psychiatric diagnosis

- 10 cards with symmetrical inkblots

- Subjects see one card at a time and are asked what they are reminded of

- Interpretation based upon
  - Common sense
  - Psychoanalytic theory
  - Rorshach's previous research and his own conclusions

Interpreting the Rorshach Inkblot Test

- **Viewing the card as a whole**
  - Reflects the ability to organize material

- **Viewing parts of the card**
  - Interest in specifics or concrete things/common sense intelligence

- **Reading in movement**
  - Human movement depicts high mental functioning and creativity
  - Animal movement depicts sexual and aggressive behaviors that society condemns
  - Movement of inanimate objects depicts tension and conflict

- **Reading in a popular response**
  - Indicates conformity

- **Certain patterns of responding reveal psychopathology**

Interpreting the TAT Test

- Series of cards with pictures on them

- Subject is asked to tell a story about what they see

- Psychologist assumes that a story's main character is the story teller and his life or someone very close to him/her
  - It reflects the storytellers preoccuptions, concerns, wishes and needs

- TAT is particularly effective in measuring <u>achievement motivation</u>

Defining Normal and Abnormal

- Medical Sciences and normality
  - The integrity of structure and function of an organ or other body part

- Psychology and normality
  - Statistical criterion
  - Ideal Mental Health criterion
  - Clinical criterion

Defining Normality

- <u>Statistical Criterion</u>
  - What most people do is normal; any deviation from the majority is abnormal

- Drawbacks
  - Specific to time and place
  - Does not distinguish between desirable and undesirable deviation from the norm

Defining Normality

- <u>Ideal Mental Health Criterion</u>
  - Normality is a goal or ideal that one strives for

- Drawback
  - Differs from theorist to theorist

Defining Normality

- <u>Clinical Criterion</u>
  - The absence of abnormal symptoms; the amount of subjective unhappiness or degree of social maladjustment a person experiences

- Drawbacks
  - Depends on individual clinicians interpretation
  - Treats psychological disorder as if it was analogous to physical disease

Thomas Szasz "The Myth of Mental Illness"

- Mental disorders are "problems in living" which in the final analysis are solvable only by the person who encounters them

- We make up words to describe people who are different...words which then allow us to lock them away

- Mental institutions are a place for people that you really don't understand, you really don't care about, and you really have little compassion for.

David Rosenhan
"On Being Sane in Insane Places"

- Designed a clever study to examine the difficulty that people have shedding the "mentally ill" label

- Rosenhan and seven associates had themselves committed to different mental hospitals by complaining that they were hearing voices

- Once admitted, they acted normal, but none of the staff noticed

- Their sanity was never detected but they were eventually released as "in remission".

- Labels are so powerful that they profoundly affect the way information is processed and perceived.

The Concept of Adjustment

- **Understanding the concept of adjustment**

- **Four main areas of adjustment**

  - **Physical**
  - **Psychological**
  - **Social**
  - **Moral**

The Concept of Adjustment

- **Who defines maladjustment?**

  - <u>Physicians</u> define it for physical disorder

  - <u>The courts</u> define it for social maladjustment

  - <u>The clergy</u> define maladjustment for the moral realm

  - <u>Psychologists</u> and psychiatrists define behavioral maladjustment

---

Defining Maladjustment

- In general, a clinician will apply the label of maladjusted to a person:

  - Who is uncomfortable

  - Who is unhappy with his/her inner life

  - Who has difficulty with interpersonal relationships

  - Who has difficulty performing the tasks expected of them

  - Whose actions appear bizarre

Diagnostic and Statistical Manual of Mental Disorders (DSM)

- The DSM classification scheme is descriptive rather than explanatory, meaning it is not based on a particular theory

- Diagnoses are based on observable symptoms and the DSM provides directions concerning the number, duration, and severity of symptoms that are necessary to assign a particular diagnosis

---

The Five Axes of the DSM

- Axis 1: Clinical disorders

  - Symptoms that cause distress or significantly impair social or occupational functioning

The Five Axes of the DSM

- Axis 2: Personality disorders and mental retardation

  - Chronic and enduring problems that generally persist throughout life and impair interpersonal and occupational functioning

The Five Axes of the DSM

- Axis 3: General medical condition

  - Physical disorders that may be relevant to understanding or treating a psychological disorder

The Five Axes of the DSM

- Axis 4: Psychosocial and environmental problems

  - Problems (such as interpersonal stressors and negative life events) that may affect the diagnosis, treatment, and prognosis of psychological disorders

The Five Axes of the DSM

- Axis 5: Global assessment of functioning

  - The individual's overall level of functioning in social, occupational, and leisure activities

DSM: Anxiety Based Disorders: Neuroses

- Fearing of urges, thoughts, feelings
- Anxiety is the root cause
- Ineffective repression
- Major symptoms
  - Takes time to develop
  - In touch with reality but it is troubled reality
  - Depression and mood swings
  - Bodily symptoms including headache, sweating, muscle tightness, heart palpitation

DSM: Anxiety Based Disorders Neuroses

- Major subtypes of neuroses

  - Phobias:
    - Neurotic anxiety is focused on a particular object or situation

  - Obsessions and compulsions:
    - A person totally preoccupied with recurrent thoughts and actions that can't be banished

  - Hysteria:
    - Collection of physical symptoms that exist without an actual organic basis

DSM—Anxiety Based Disorders Psychoses

- A neurotic is emotionally crippled but still "slugs it out with life"

- When fear reaches an intense level such that a <u>person withdraws completely from life</u>, that person is labeled psychotic

- A neurotic attempts to deal with tensions and anxieties while a psychotic individual gives up

DSM—Anxiety Based Disorders: Psychoses

- <u>Schizophrenia</u>: severe disturbances in intellectual, emotional, and perceptual senses of self and others

  - <u>Simple</u>: slow reduction in external attachments and interests, interpersonal relations whither. They are left apathetic and indifferent

  - <u>Hebephrenic</u>: severe personality disintegration; popular stereotype of insanity

  - <u>Catatonic</u>: patients are mute and preoccupied with a stream of consciousness

  - <u>Paranoid</u>: convinced that others are plotting against them

DSM—Anxiety Based Disorders: Psychoses

- <u>Affective Reactions</u>: Mood disorders in which people are excessively happy or unhappy, optimistic or pessimistic, manic or depressed

  - <u>Manic reactions</u>: increasing agitation, excitement, and deteriorating judgment in relationships with others

  - <u>Depressive reactions</u>: depression and mania alternate with each other over long periods of time

DSM—Personality Disorders

- Neuroses and psychoses come about as an attempt to control anxiety

- <u>Personality disorders</u> do not result from anxiety

- <u>Personality disorders</u> are usually marked by a limited capacity to adapt to the social environment and by an inability to establish a rational, stable, rewarding relationship with the others

DSM—Personality Disorders

- Two major subtypes

  - <u>Anti-social personality</u>: Misbehaves socially without guilt; incapable of forming lasting affectionate bonds.

  - Special case of the *psychopath*:
    - Egocentric and narcissistic
    - Impulsive and irresponsible
    - can't tolerate everyday frustrations
    - poor judgment
    - seeks immediate gratification

  - <u>Sexual deviance</u>: When sexual behavior is compulsive, destructive, accompanied by great anxiety, guilt, or causes discomfort

DSM—Organic Disorders

- Many types of behavior disorders can be traced directly to:

  - Damage to the brain

  - An imbalance in hormones or neurotransmitters

  - Genetic influences

DSM—Organic Disorders

- **Melancholia**

  - Severe depression with the onset of menopause

  - A woman loses her sexual desire and believes she is no longer attractive

  - Estrogen involvement

DSM—Organic Disorders

- **Stroke based behavior disorders**

  - A blood vessel breaks in the brain and a person loses control of one or both sides of their body

  - Results in
    - confusion,
    - forgetfulness
    - hallucinations

DSM—Organic Disorders

- **Senile psychosis**

  - "hardening of the arteries"

  - blood supply to the brain is choked off

  - Severe cognitive disintegration

  - Patient lapses into a child-like stat

DSM—Organic Disorders

- **Alzheimer's disease**

  - Severe cognitive disintegration
  - Symptoms are similar to senile psychosis
  - Associated with degeneration of the <u>hippocampus</u> and cerebral cortex
  - Buildup of <u>amyloid plaques</u> and <u>neurofibrillary tangles</u>..disruption of normal protein production
  - Associated with reduction in the neurotransmitter acetylcholine
  - Associated with a defect in the 21st chromosome

DSM—Organic Disorders

- **Venereal disease**

  - Germs associated with syphilis attack the brain and cause a general paresis (paralysis)

  - Cognitive deficits in advanced stages

DSM—Organic Disorders

- **Alcohol addiction disorder**

  - Denial
  - Aggressive behavior
  - Neglect of physical appearance
  - Impaired memory and forgetting
  - Liver disease
  - Brain changes
  - Genetic linkage

DSM—Organic Disorders

• **Manic-depression**

  –**Genetic linkage**

    • Monozygotic twins share a 50% concordance rate.

    • Dizygotic twins, brothers, sisters or children share a concordance rate of only 5-10%

DSM—Organic Disorders

• Schizophrenia

  – dopamine hypothesis of schizophrenia suggests that schizophrenia results from excess activity at dopamine synapses in certain areas of the brain

  – glutamate hypothesis of schizophrenia suggests the problem relates partially to deficient activity at glutamate receptors.

  – Some studies implicate frontal cortex

  – Genetic linkage

The Epidemiology of Behavior Disorder

• **Demographic Variability**

  • Gender

    – More males than females in state, county and VA hospitals

    – Higher incidence of brain syndromes, alcoholism, drug addiction and sexual deviation in males than females

    – Higher incidence of psychoses and neuroses in females than males

The Epidemiology of Behavior Disorder

• **Demographic Variability**

  • Age

    –Neuroses, antisocial personalities and personality disorders peak in adolescence

    –Schizophrenia and other psychoses, alcoholism peak in middle age

    –Organic syndromes peak in old age

The Epidemiology of Behavior Disorder

• **Demographic Variability**

  • Marital status

    –Highest rates of mental disorder seen in separated and divorced individuals

    –Lowest rates of mental disorder seen in married men and woman

The Epidemiology of Behavior Disorder

• **Demographic Variability**

  – Social class

    • Lower the social stratum, the higher the incidence of mental illness

    • High socioeconomic class is associated with high levels of neuroses

    • Low socioeconomic class is associated with high levels of psychoses

The Epidemiology of Behavior Disorder

• **Demographic Variability**

    – Cross cultural variability

        • Prevalence of mental disorder in all cultures but the symptomatic expression and way it is interpreted may differ from culture to culture

---

The Epidemiology of Behavior Disorder

• **Demographic Variability**

    • Ethnic group

        – No differences across ethic group

Institutional Approaches to the Treatment of Behavior Disorders

In the last decade of the 20th century, Dr. Philippe Pinel, a French physician, instituted dramatic changes in the treatment of those suffering from mental illness

Pinel put into practice his strong belief that those suffering from mental illness should be treated with compassion.

They should not be put in prisons and put into chains along with people who were unable to earn a living or pay their debts to society

---

Moral Care in Small Asylums in the 1800s

• Emphasis on:

    – Inspirational classes
    – Frequent religious services
    – Work was encouraged
    – Frequent group meetings
    – Frequent individual meetings with staff
    – Goal was to establish regular habits of self control

• Remarkable results

    – 75% of patients recovered
    – 58% never had a relapse

Moral Care in Small Asylums Replaced by Custodial Care in Large Psychiatric Hospitals

• Great influx of emigrants to the US quadrupled the client-doctor ratio

• Many large state hospitals were built but staffing was done by political appointment

    – Staff were often untrained and uncaring

• Studies during the early 1950s showed that most patients did absolutely nothing during a typical day

• Staff would only respond and give attention to pathological symptoms

---

The Advent of Drugs in the 1950s

• Tranquilizers and antidepressants became available for the first time

• Negative symptoms can be eliminated and patients will be easier to work with

• Drugs reduce symptoms but often they don't get at the underlying causes of behavior disorders

Max Jones and the Therapeutic Community of the 60s and 70s

- Patients ordinarily receive only 1 hour of therapy a day…too much time is wasted

- Patients are not helpless, hopeless or irresponsible…they can collaborate with staff in directing their own therapy

- <u>The goal</u>: Promote interactions with others and build confidence

- Physical changes in hospitals were dramatic
  - Doors were unlocked
  - Patients started to wear their own clothing
  - Meals were served family style
  - Bedrooms took on the appearance of homes
  - Patients confronted and supported each other

Community Mental Health Programs of the 80s and 90s

- Establishment of <u>halfway houses</u>

- Therapy is provided without isolating the patient from their home environment

- Patient can work during the day and return to the halfway home in the evening

- <u>Goal</u>: Shift care away from large psychiatric hospitals to local clinics

- Political and social climate has influenced funding

- NIMN (not in my neighborhood) attitude

The Three Basic Forms of Therapy

- **Insight therapies**
  - Psychoanalysis
  - Psychodynamic
  - Cognitive
    - Rational emotive therapy
  - Humanistic
    - Client centered therapy
  - Group, family, and marital

The Three Basic Forms of Therapy

- **Behavior therapies**
  - Classical conditioning
    - Systematic desensitization
    - Aversion therapy
  - Operant conditioning
    - Shaping
    - Reinforcement
    - Punishment
    - Extinction
  - Observational learning
    - Modeling

The Three Basic Forms of Therapy

- Biomedical therapies

  - Psychopharmacology

  - Electroconvulsive shock

  - Psychosurgery

Questions Which Must be Asked of Any Therapy

- What is the cure rate?

- How reliable is it and does it work all the time?

- What are the side effects?

- How do you define cure?

Electroconvulsive Shock Therapy

•Electroconvulsive therapy (ECT) is an electrically induced seizure that is used for the treatment of severe depression.

•Used with patients who have not responded to antidepressant medication or are suicidal.

•Applied every other day for a period of two weeks.

•Side effects include damage to the brain, liver, and lungs as well as memory loss.
   •Memory loss can be minimized if shock is   localized to the right hemisphere.

Psychosurgery: Lobotomy

•Cutting of the frontal lobes can produce the following:

   •   High fatality rate

   •   Patients can be left emotionally flat

   •   Patients are unable to think about the past or future

•Performed today as a last resort

Tranquilizers

- • __Examples__: reserpine, valium

- • __Disorders__: schizophrenia

- • __Action__: alters dopamine

- • __Influence__: calming effect on behavior

Antidepressants

- • __Examples__: imipramine, Prozac

- • __Disorders__: depression and manic-depression

- • __Action__: serotonin reuptake and dopamine synthesis

- • __Influence__: elevates mood/reverses depression

Antipsychotics

- • __Examples__: Lithium, Chlorpromazine

- • __Disorders__: psychoses

- • __Action__: dopamine synthesis

- • __Influence__: reduces hallucinations

Hormones

- • __Examples__: estrogen (E), depoprovera

- • __Disorders__: mood and sexual disorders

- • __Action__: dopamine and serotonin

- • __Influence__: E reduces mood disorders while depoprovera reduces sexual cravings in males

Some Major Issues to Consider with Drug Therapies

- Side effects
  - Tardive dyskenesia

- Alternatives (e.g., herbs)
  - St. John's Wort

- Symptom removal only?

- Overmedication

Insight or Intrapsychic Therapies: Psychoanalytic Therapy

- Get rid of underlying problem..not just symptoms
  - Look to the future
  - Look in the past

- Many different forms but most depend upon:
  - Transference.....the "father figure"
  - Free Association....everything you do is represented in conflict

- Criteria for successful patients
  - Bright
  - Verbal
  - Self motivated
  - Willingness to cooperate

- Works best with mildly neurotic patients

Carl Rogers Client-Centered Therapy

- Patient, not therapist, determines outcome of therapy

- Emphasize conscious determinants of behavior

- Focus on ideal state that patient wants to achieve

- Mirror the patient

- Give unconditional positive regard

- Be supportive

Rational Emotive Therapy (RET): Albert Ellis

- (A) Activating event
  - Individual is blocked from desired goal

- (B) Irrational beliefs
  - Individual interprets the frustration in an irrational erroneous manner

- (C) Emotional consequences
  - Individual experiences negative feelings which reinforce the original irrational beliefs

- (D) Disputed irrational beliefs
  - Individual challenges irrational beliefs, which change negative emotions

The Eysenck Report
Are Insight Therapies Really That Effective?

- Percent of mildly neurotic patients improving following:

  - Insight treatment   44%

  - Any other treatment   64%

  - No treatment   72%

Factors Influencing the Outcome of Insight Therapy

- Therapist variables
  - Empathy, genuineness, experience

- Client variables
  - Nature of problem, client motivation

- Techniques
  - Timing of interpretations, specific techniques

Improvement and Satisfaction With Insight Therapy

- Problem improvement...patients said:
  - 42% said they were helped a lot
  - 44% said they were helped somewhat
  - 14% said they were not helped

- Therapy satisfaction...patients said:
  - 62% said they were very/completely satisfied
  - 27% said they were fairly satisfied
  - 11% said they were not satisfied

Group Therapies

- Factors outside the patient are responsible for behavior disorder

- Mental disorder is caused by a disruption of social relationships

- It is not due to a disruption in personality or biological changes

- Best therapy is:
  - Change the patient's social environment
  - Change how the people in the patient's social environment treat the patient

History of Group Therapy

- Earliest form was Greek Dramas

  - Bull sessions
  - Prayer meetings
  - Revivals

- Boston physician J.H. Pratt was the first to use group therapy with tuberculosis patients

Techniques of Group Therapy

- Jerome Frank, a leading group therapist, believes that all group therapies have in common the following:

  - Intimate sharing of feelings, experiences, and ideas

  - An atmosphere of mutual respect and understanding

  - Overall goal of helping a person to develop self respect and a deeper self-understanding

Types of Group Therapy: Formal Groups

- One definite formal leader who has well organized plan for the group

- Goal: Break down psychological resistance

- Works well with psychotic and withdrawn patients

Types of Group Therapy: Inspirational Groups

- Examples of Inspirational Groups
  - Alcoholics Anonymous (AA)
  - 7th Step Foundation for Ex Convicts
  - Weight Watchers

- Heavily reliant upon emotional devices and a strong leader

- Works best for addiction based disorders

Types of Group Therapy:
Psychodrama

- Developed by Jacob Moreno
- Therapists serve as the "director"
- Patient serves as "hero" or "heroine"
- A "play" takes place on a real stage and centers around some problem in the patient's life
- Trained "actor-therapists" assist
- Facilitates increased communication
- Audience (other patients) can also benefit by seeing problems similar to their own presented on stage

Types of Group Therapy
Transactional Analysis (TA)

- Form of role playing developed by Eric Berne
- "Game" is the stereo-typed and misleading interpersonal "transactions" that people adopt when communicating with each other
- Each game that you play is part of an overall "script" that a person uses in performing various roles in his or her life
- Goal of TA: Get a person to consciously change their behavior so they no longer engage in unconscious and superficial role playing
- Patients are trained to distinguish between ego states: "parent", "adult", "child".

Types of Group Therapy:
Encounter Groups

- Many different varieties
- People who have had little previous contact with each other
- Group may meet one or more times a week
- Members may live with one another in close contact for a day, week, or longer
- Goal: to bring feelings out into the open, strip away defenses, communicate more honestly
- Success comes from
  - Giving maximum support to each group member
  - Each group member must confront each other with their faults, delusions, and excuses

Does Group Therapy Work?

- Most studies show the following mixed results:
  - 1/3 get better
  - 1/3 get worse
  - 1/3 are unchanged immediately after
- Few differences among various types of group therapy in their effectiveness
- Primary benefit: Immediately after the experience , 65% of patients report that it was a positive one

Behavior Therapy

- Mental illness is thought to be caused by unhealthy living conditions, not character defects or mental weakness
- Society has failed to teach people healthy behaviors
- Best form of treatment is to put a patient in a new milieu...a new social environment... to help patient learn better habits of adjustment
- Like a non-stop 24 hour a day encounter group
- Draw the patient into normal relationships, build their confidence, and social competence

Behavior Therapies:
Aversion Therapy for Drinking

- **Before conditioning**
  - UCS (nausea producing drug) produces UCR (nausea)
- **During conditioning**
  - UCS (drug) + neutral stimulus (alcoholic drink) produces UCR (nausea)
- **After conditioning**
  - CS (alcoholic drink without drug) produces CR (nausea)

Systematic Desensitization

- Construction of a hierarchy of fears (from most feared to least feared) for a person fearful of driving on a busy expressway on a rainy night

  - Driving on a busy expressway on a rainy night (most feared)
  - Driving on a busy expressway in the daytime
  - Driving on the same street at night
  - Driving on the same street in the rain
  - Driving along a busy street on a sunny day
  - Driving along an empty, quiet street on a sunny day
  - Sitting behind the wheel of a nonmoving car in the driveway (least feared)

Token Economies

- Grew out of the frequent observation that a child-like dependency is created in many state hospitals because patients are given everything they need

- "Institutional neuroses" develops and patients stop caring

- Goal is to encourage responsibility

- Staff are directed to:
  - reinforce socially approved and healthy behaviors
  - ignore "inappropriate" or "abnormal" behavior

Do Token Economies Work?

- Very reliable behavioral changes are produced with a wide variety of disorders (mild to severe) and a range of ages in patients.

- Probably the single most effective therapy in producing reliable change

Key Issues in Social Psychology Experiments

- **The ethics of deception**
  - Information frequently is withheld from subjects
  - Is the withholding of information ethical?
- **Risk versus reward**
  - Is the information gained from an experiment that involves deception worth the risk that it may cause harm to the subjects
- **Use of confederates or stooges**
  - Some subjects in social psychological research are actually part of the experimenter's research team. They give false or deceptive information so as to mislead subjects in the experiment

Evolution of Social Psychology and Conformity and Obedience Studies

- Did the German people represent an unusually sadistic race of people or, instead, are all people, regardless of race, capable of committing unspeakable acts because the power of the situation is so overwhelming?

Kurt Lewin - 1939 The Father of Social Psychology

- Lewin's research emerged at a time when the social-political structure of Nazi Germany permitted a dominant leader like Adolph Hitler

- Lewin and his research team assigned school children to one of three groups that contained an *authoritarian, democratic or laissez-fair* leader.

- The children were led in an arts and crafts project. The behavior of the children was studied in response to the different leadership styles.

How do Leadership Styles Influence Followers?

- **Democratic leadership**
  - Encouraged and assisted the group's decision making
  - Highest levels of motivation and originality
- **Autocratic leadership**
  - Made all the decisions for the group
  - Boys worked the hardest but only when leader was watching
  - More aggressive and hostile and more submission to leader
- **Laissez Faire leadership**
  - Complete freedom with no guidance
  - Total Chaos
- **Leadership styles and not personalities were the most important factor**

Solomon Asch and the Phenomenon of Conformity

- **Conformity means altering your behavior to match other people's behavior or expectations**

- **The pressure to conform often exerts an overwhelming coercive experience**

Even Our Most Obvious Observations Can be Manipulated

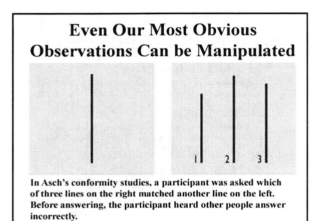

In Asch's conformity studies, a participant was asked which of three lines on the right matched another line on the left. Before answering, the participant heard other people answer incorrectly.

The Subjects in Asch's Experiment

Three of the participants in Asch's experiments on conformity. The one in the middle looking uncomfortable is the real subject. The others are the experimenter's confederates.

Impact of the Size of the Incorrect Majority

Asch found that conformity became more frequent as group size increased to about three and then it leveled off.

Impact of Unanimity

In Asch's experiments, participants who were faced with a unanimous incorrect majority conformed on 32% of trials. Participants who had one ally giving the correct answer were less likely to conform.

Milgram Obedience Studies

- Stanley Milgram asked "What are the factors contributing to the sometimes blind compliance that people will show in response to the demands of an authority figure even though it may be against our ethics and sense of right and wrong".

- Obedience is defined as "compliance to the commands of an authority figure"

Milgram Obedience Studies

- The famous British historian C.P. Snow said:
  - "When you think of the long and gloomy history of man, you will find more hideous crimes committed in the name of obedience than have been committed in the name of rebellion"
- How can these atrocities be explained?
  - The massacres at My Lai during the Vietnam War
  - The holocaust of World War II
  - The genocide in Darfur

Milgram Obedience Studies

- Migram's experiment involved deception.

- Subjects were told that they were participating in a study examining the influence of punishment on learning.

- The "teacher", the true subject in the experiment, was to punish with electric shocks, the "learner" who was asked to remember word pairs and was a confederate of the experimenter

Milgram Obedience Studies

- Example of word pairs: tree-limb

  - Tree
    1. Limb
    2. Rock
    3. House
    4. Car

  .

The Milgram Obedience Studies

Room A	Room B
T S. M.	L

T = Teacher
L = Learner
S. M. = Stanley Milgram

Milgram Obedience Studies

- The shock voltage increased with each incorrect answer.

- In reality, no shocks were being administered to the "learner".

- The "learner" in the adjacent room was acting like he was in pain…. He was the confederate or stooge.

- The experimenter, Stanley Milgram, sternly told the "teachers" to go on even though the "learner" was pounding on the wall faking that he was in great pain.

Milgram Obedience Studies

- **The results of the studied showed:**
  - 26 of the 40 "teachers" in the experiment went to the end of the shock generator panel and delivered the most intense shocks

- **Characteristics of the teachers:**
  - They were not sadists, they showed extreme tension and anxiety and frequently said that they wanted to stop

Milgram Obedience Studies

- **What accounts for the obedience?**
  - Everyone learns that in certain situations they must do as they are told
    - A policeman stopping someone who is speeding
    - A doctor who tells you to undress for a physical

- **We assume that an authority figure knows what they are doing even though it may run against our morals and ethics.**

The Milgram Obedience Studies: Experimenter Giving Phone Commands

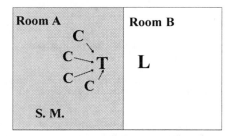

= Teacher   S. M. = Stanley Milgram
L = Learner

The Milgram Obedience Studies: Type of Feedback from Learner

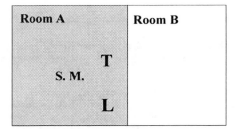

T = Teacher   S. M. = Stanley Milgram
L = Learner

Milgram Obedience Studies: Social Support for Disobedience or Approval

T = Teacher   S. M. = Stanley Milgram
L = Learner   C = Confederate

Importance of Milgram's Studies

- Most controversial studies ever conducted in psychology. Of interest to
  - Political scientists
  - Historians
  - Philosophers
  - Sociologists

- 1974 book, *Obedience to Authority*

- <u>Major interest</u>: 2/3 of the "teachers" went to the end of the shock generator panel and administered the most intense shocks

Attack on Milgram Studies

- Psychologist Diana Baumrind attacked Milgram's results for the emotional stress, tension, and loss of dignity it caused the subjects

- Milgram noted that he did not set out to create stress in the subjects

- Milgram believed that what disturbed people was the results, not the methods

Milgram Studies Increased Sensitivity to Ethical Issues in Research

- Establishment of ethical guidelines and safeguards by the APA and federal government regarding experiments involving human subjects

Questions Must Still Be Asked

- Was the extreme deception unethical?

- Did the dramatic and unexpected results justify the emotional stress?

- Could less deceptive methods be used and still get the same results?

- Under what conditions are deception justified?

Part IV. Practice Exams and Quizzes

PRACTICE EXAM #1

1. In evolutionary terms, the most advanced portion of the brain is the:
    a. cerebellum
    b. cerebrum
    c. synapse
    d. input area

2. Phrenology is:
    a. the study of how bumps on the head relate to behavior
    b. an early name of psychology
    c. the study of deviant behavior attributed to brain and heart tissue
    d. the study of surgical experiments of the brain

3. The "father" of experimental psychology is
    a. Sir Francis Gall
    b. Charles Darwin
    c. James McConnell
    d. None of the above

4. One way to prevent experimental bias is to:
    a. use a dependent variable
    b. manipulate the independent variable
    c. use a double-blind procedure
    d. use a placebo

5. Surveys frequently are inaccurate because they fail to include:
    a. proper control groups
    b. placebos
    c. representative samples
    d. none of the above

6. According to Robert Rosenthall, the self-fulfilling prophecy refers to the fact that
    a. an experimenter in an animal laboratory can unknowingly influence the behavior of his animals
    b. an experimenter conducting human research can unconsciously influence the behavior of his subjects
    c. periods of REM sleep can be induced by prayer
    d. a and b

7. Phineas Gage's change in personality was due to damage to his:
   a. hippocampus
   b. amygdala
   c. frontal cortex
   d. hypothalamus

8. In the typical psychological experiment, the responses made by the subjects are called:
   a. the dependent variable
   b. the intervening variable
   c. the independent variable
   d. the co-dependent variable

9. Which of the following is an "applied setting"?
   a. a lab set up to study sleep disorders
   b. a field station set up to study maternal behavior in monkeys
   c. a psychology department in a state college
   d. a rape crisis center

10. The ultimate goal of psychology is to:
    a. discover the causes of behavior
    b. explore the human psyche
    c. solve the problems of humankind
    d. understand human behavior

11. The story of Phineus Gage is important to psychology because:
    a. It illustrated the importance of introspection
    b. It showed that philosophy was the basis of psychology
    c. It showed how changes in the brain produced changes in behavior
    d. It illustrated that water can serve as a placebo

12. Chlorpromazine and reserpine have both been proven useful in treating schizophrenia. Both drugs act on:
    a. acetylcholine and oxytocin systems
    b. norepinehrine and dopamine systems
    c. prolactin and growth hormone systems
    d. acetylcholine and dopamine systems
    e. norepinephrine nad oxytocin systems

13. The subfield of psychology whose primary goals include the study of the workplace is called_____psychology.
    a. organizational
    b. community
    c. health
    d. consumer

14. Descartes argued that:
    a. the pineal body is the physical housing for the mind
    b. mind and matter interact
    c. the mind is made of ordinary matter
    d. dualism explains the origins of the mind

15. Broca's research suggested that damage to the _____ causes deficits in _____.
    a. front part of the brain; tasting
    b. rear of the brain; seeing
    c. right side of the brain; hearing
    d. left side of the brain; speaking

16. Psychology began in _____ in the _____.
    a. Germany; late 19th century
    b. France; middle 19th century
    c. England; early 20th century
    d. The United States; early 19th century

17. Your psychology professor's research has show that female mice developing in utero between two male mice_____ than female mice that develop between two female mice.
    a. are less aggressive
    b. have larger brains
    c. are more aggressive
    d. have smaller brains

18. If a researcher is measuring the length of time different couples were engaged before getting married and their reported level of happiness with their marriage, in order to determine whether these two variables are related, he or she is carrying out a(n) _____ study.
    a. experimental
    b. correlational
    c. naturalistic observation
    d. case

19. One example of a theory that cannot be subjected to rigorous scientific testing is:
    a. Einstein's theory of relativity
    b. Helmholt's theory (doctrine) of specific nerve energies
    c. Freud's theory of psychosexual development
    d. Pavlov's theory of classical conditioning

20. The variable that is measured in an experiment is called the_____ variable.
    a. relational
    b. independent
    c. causal
    d. dependent

21. Dr. Thomas is conducting a study on reaction time. He allows subjects to exercise strenuously for either 0, 10, or 20 minutes. Next, subjects are seated at a table containing a red push button and a yellow light. Each subject is asked to push the button as soon as he or she sees the light flash. Dr. Thomas measures the time it takes each subject to push the button after the light is lit. What is the independent variable in this study?
    a. exercise
    b. the amount of time spent exercising
    c. the button
    d. the light

22. Your psychology professor's research shows that prenatal stress in mice has a tendency to:
    a. promote homosexual behavior
    b. reduce activity
    c. elevate aggression and activity
    d. alter aggression

23. An operational definition:
    a. is a technique used to measure a dependent variable
    b. guarantees that all subjects in a study will be treated equally
    c. describes a variable in terms of the operations that will be used to measure or manipulate it
    d. of most variables is difficult to achieve in psychology because most psychological research involves hypothetical constructs concerning the nature of thinking and emotion

24. Counterbalancing is used in experimental research to:
    a. make the number of subjects in the experimental and control groups equal
    b. prevent order effects from influencing the dependent variable
    c. control for differences among subject variables
    d. make statistical analysis of the date simpler

25. Dr. Smith's research often involves observation of children interacting with their parents. During these observations, the number of times that the child smiles and frowns in response to parental instructions is counted. One problem encountered by Dr. Smith in this type of research is:
    a. the difficulty in counterbalancing the order of stimulus presentation
    b. insuring that subjects are randomly assigned to groups
    c. performing a statistical analysis of the results
    d. the subjectivity that may be present in measuring the dependent variable.

26. In essence, random assignment means that:
    a. each subject in the study has an equal chance of being assigned to either the control group or the experimental group.
    b. Subjects with particular characteristics are eliminated from the study
    c. Subjects with particular characteristics are assigned to particular groups
    d. Neither the subject nor the experimenter is aware of to which groups the subjects have been assigned, and thus do not know which group will be exposed to the independent variable

27. Emile Carcaro's research with Prozac shows that:
    a. sex behavior is diminished after 3 weeks of treatment
    b. the drug has no effect on personality disorders
    c. the drug reduces violent outbursts such as road rage
    d. none of the above

28. Your psychology professor's research showed that C57BL/6J female mice exhibit very little aggressive behavior during pregnancy while DBA/2J female mice are very aggressive while pregnant. The author concluded that this difference was probably due to strain differences in:
    a. maternal environment
    b. prolactin secretion
    c. neural progesterone sensitivity
    d. jaw size

29. Dr. Jones' research involves in-depth analyses of two subjects in order to learn how a tragedy in their hometown affected their attitudes about success in life. Dr. Jones' research is an example of a(n):
   a. case study
   b. experiment
   c. correlational study based on naturalistic observation
   d. experiment involving a retrospective analysis

30. Although animal rights activists target animal research, it is clear that
   a. animal researchers have largely ignored them
   b. they do so merely for publicity
   c. they do so merely for the money involved
   d. pets are more often abused than are animals used in research

31. The addition of a control group:
   a. permits a contrast between manipulating the independent variable and no treatment
   b. increases the validity of the operational definition
   c. works best with human subjects
   d. assures a random sample of subjects

32. One of the drawbacks of the case study is that:
   a. subjects may serve as their own controls
   b. the dependent variables are always confounded
   c. subjects cannot remain anonymous
   d. subjects may not be representative of the population as a whole

33. Tissue samples and computer simulation are turning out be useful substitutes for carrying out research with live animals:
   a. True
   b. False

34. The procedure in which animals are deliberately mated to produce offspring with certain characteristics is called_____selection:
   a. natural
   b. artificial
   c. contrived
   d. synthetic

35. Research by Bob Bridges on maternal behavior in rats shows that:
    a. oxytocin reduces maternal responses
    b. serotonin promotes attachment
    c. dopamine causes female rats to eat their young
    d. none of the above

36. An organism's phenotype is the result of:
    a. its genotype
    b. the influence of environmental influences and experiences
    c. the interaction of its genotype with the environment
    d. the reproductive success of its parents

37. Factors that appear to have been responsible for the evolution of our species include
    a. increases in brain size
    b. encephalization
    c. the ability to walk upright
    d. all of the above

38. Fraternal twins occur when:
    a. two eggs are fertilized by the same sperm
    b. two sperm fertilize the same egg
    c. a fertilized ovum divides
    d. two different sperm fertilize two different ova

39. A special diet is instrumental in saving the lives of children who have:
    a. Down's syndrome
    b. Huntington's chorea
    c. PKU
    d. XYY syndrome

40. Your introductory psychology professor has conducted research examining
    a. spreading depression and memory
    b. the development of language in chimpanzees
    c. the effects of fetal alcohol exposure on social behavior
    d. the relationship between hormones and social behavior in rodents

41. Twin studies of alcohol use and alcoholism have show that
    a. females are more likely than males to inherit a predisposition for alcoholism
    b. concordance rates for alcoholism in both MZ and DZ twins is low
    c. males are more likely than females to become binge drinkers
    d. concordance rates for both of these variables is higher for MZ twins than for DZ twins

42. The reproductive strategy in which parental investment is shared, but always equal is::
    a. monogamy
    b. polygyny
    c. polyandry
    d. polygynandry

43. Carol Sue Carter's research on voles is important because it suggest that:
    a. maternal behavior may be related to the production of substance P
    b. aggression may be related to dopamine
    c. sex behavior may be related to dopamine
    d. maternal behavior may be related to the production of oxytocin

44. According to the idea of kin selection, you are more likely to behave altruistically toward:
    a. a brother over a sister
    b. a cousin over a brother
    c. any sibling over your parents
    d. a sister over a cousin

45. The idea that the group to which one belongs is superior to all other groups to which one does not belong is called:
    a. racism
    b. discrimination
    c. prejudice
    d. ethnocentrism

46. A child whose natural parents are alcoholics has:
    a. An increased risk of alcoholism
    b. An increased risk of alcoholism only if raised by the natural parents
    c. No increased risk of alcoholism if raised by the natural parents
    d. No increased alcoholism regardless of the home environment

47. An animal breeder often uses natural selection to produce specific characteristics in the animals he or she is breeding.
    a. True
    b. False

48. According to your introductory psychology professor, research in psychology often involves:
    a. accidental discoveries and frequent failures
    b. collaboration from other scientists and graduate students
    c. federal grant money to underwrite research costs
    d. costly equipment and technical support
    e. all of the above

49. The axon carries messages toward the:
    a. soma
    b. terminal buttons
    c. dendrites
    d. mitochondria

50. The neuron that is excited or inhibited by the transmitter substances released by another neuron is called the_____ neuron.
    a. synaptic
    b. receiving
    c. presynaptic
    d. postsynaptic

51. John has consumed a drug that retards the rate of reuptake. This will have the effect of:
    a. prolonging the effects of the transmitter substance
    b. diminishing the effects of the transmitter substance
    c. closing the ion channels
    d. blocking the receptor molecules of the postsynaptic neuron

52. The presence of opioids in the brain would be favored by natural selection because they:
    a. make successful reproduction more likely
    b. ensure that a hungry animal eats
    c. ensure a thirsty animal drinks
    d. make sleep occur during time of extreme fatigue

53. Your psychology professor's research on aggressive behavior in female mice may be important for:
    a. destroying the myth that only males are innately aggressive
    b. a and c
    c. understanding mood changes in humans
    d. none of the above

54. Allison is a very talented gymnast. According to most modern psychologists, her skill in this area most likely represents:
    a. a genetic predisposition
    b. environmental influences
    c. her desire to excel in the sport
    d. the interaction of genetic and environmental factors

55. A major finding in Rosenzweig's research is that rats reared in enriched environments, compared to rats reared in impoverished environments, tended to have:
    a. thicker cerebral cortices and a better blood supply to the brain
    b. increased levels of serotonin
    c. dense capillaries in their visual cortex
    d. extensive synaptic connections throughout their endocrine system

56. The large bundle of axons that links the two cerebral hemispheres is called the:
    a. raphe nucleus
    b. medial forebrain bundle
    c. corpus callosum
    d. congealed gyrus

57. After falling off her bicycle and hitting her head on the pavement, Alice cannot move her right leg and arm. As a result of her accident, she may have sustained serious damage to her_____lobe.
    a. right parietal
    b. left parietal
    c. right frontal
    d. left frontal

58. Your psychology professor's research has shown that:
    a. female mice become very aggressive after they give birth and receive suckling stimulation from their young
    b. female mice exhibit aggression during pregnancy primarily as a result of the hormone prostaglandins
    c. the aggression of female mice is reduced when they develop ina prenatal environment that is high in testosterone
    d. prolactin is responsible for the aggression seen in postpartum mice
    e. all of the above

59. The primary principles governing human psychological research are:
    a. minimal risk, informed consent, and right to privacy
    b. informed consent, right to privacy, and absence of coercion
    c. minimal risk, informed consent, and absence of coercion
    d. right to refuse, absence of coercion, and informed consent
    e. informed consent, right to privacy, and right to refuse

60. The phenomena called "runners high" is probably related to the production of :
    a. angiotensin
    b. endorphin
    c. serotonin
    d. oxytocin
    e. none of the above

ANSWERS FOR PRACTICE EXAM #1

1. b	21. b	41. d
2. a	22. d	42. a
3. d	23. c	43. d
4. c	24. b	44. d
5. c	25. d	45. d
6. d	26. a	46. a
7. c	27. c	47. b
8. a	28. c	48. e
9. d	29. a	49. b
10. d	30. d	50. d
11. c	31. a	51. a
12. b	32. d	52. a
13. a	33. b	53. b
14. b	34. b	54. d
15. d	35. d	55. a
16. a	36. c	56. c
17. c	37. d	57. d
18. b	38. d	58. a
19. c	39. c	59. a
20. d	40. d	60. b

PRACTICE EXAM #2

1. The planarian flatworm studies on memory suggest:
   a. that memory is stored throughout the human body
   b. a chemical or molecular basis to memory
   c. that memory has no parallel in neural molecules
   d. that the quest for the engram is unwarranted

2. The serial position curve indicates that:
   a. items at the beginning of a list are stored in long-term memory
   b. items at the end of a list are stored in short-term memory
   c. items in the middle of a list are not stored in short-term memory
   d. all of the above

3. When flatworms learn to do a task and one is then cut in half
   a. only the "head" seems to remember the task
   b. only the "tail" can perform the task
   c. both sections perform the task equally well
   d. neither section can perform the task

4. Research on the "visual cliff" with a number of animal species, including the human, suggests that:
   a. depth perception is learned
   b. visual depth perception is attained along with touch
   c. visual depth perception requires little or no training
   d. at least one fall, no matter how minor, is necessary for the attainment of depth perception

5. The research by R.L. Fantz on human infants suggest that:
   a. most perception is learned
   b. flat objects are preferred over round objects
   c. there may be innate perceptual response patterns in the newborn
   d. depth and distance perception requires specific training

6. The fovea is an area on the back of the eye:
   a. where the optic nerve exits the eyes and therefore we have our best vision
   b. where there are no receptor neurons and therefore we have our best vision
   c. where rods are concentrated and therefore we have our best vision
   d. where cones are concentrated therefore we have our best vision

7. Habituation functions to:
   a. make us more responsive to novel stimuli
   b. aid us in ignoring unimportant stimuli
   c. enhance our susceptibility to classical conditioning
   d. prevent us from overreacting emotionally to important stimuli

8. Through classical conditioning, an organism learns:
   a. about reinforcing stimuli
   b. how to execute a response to obtain a reinforcer
   c. that some stimuli predict important events
   d. the three-term contingency

9. In Pavlov's original research, the dogs only salivated to the sound of the tone if the:
   a. tone followed the food powder
   b. tone was extremely loud
   c. food powder was presented soon after the tone
   d. tone and the food powder were presented at the same time

10. In classical conditioning, the stimulus that naturally elicits the reflexive behavior is called the _____ stimulus.
    a. unconditional
    b. conditional
    c. discriminative
    d. signaling

11. Any neutral stimulus paired with a stimulus such as food that elicits a response is called a(n) _____ stimulus.
    a. unconditional
    b. discriminative
    c. orienting
    d. conditional

12. When Frank was young he was stung by a bee and had a severe allergic reaction. Now, many years later, whenever he hears a buzzing sound (including when people imitate a buzzing sound), he becomes nervous and panics. In this example, the conditional response is:
    a. the bee
    b. the severe allergic reaction
    c. the buzzing sound
    d. Frank's reacting nervously and panicking

13. Which two factors influence the acquisition of a CR?
    a. UCS intensity and the temporal relationship between the CS and UCS
    b. UCS intensity and the strength of responding
    c. CS intensity and the temporal relationship between the UCR and CF
    d. UCS intensity and the temporal relationship between the CS and CR

14. Spontaneous recovery is said to occur when a:
    a. previously extinguished CR suddenly reappears after an interval of time has passed
    b. CR is elicited by a stimulus similar to the one used during acquisition training
    c. CR is elicited by one CS but not other (neutral) stimuli
    d. CR is no longer elicited by the UCS

15. Nicole was in a car accident during a rain storm. Now whenever she must drive during the rain, even when it is only a sprinkle, she gets nervous. This response is likely due to:
    a. discrimination
    b. generalization
    c. spontaneous recovery
    d. extinction

16. Several years ago you were bitten by a friend's dog. Since then you have been afraid of dogs and other animals that resemble dogs. Your reaction is an example of a(n):
    a. innate fear of animals that most people have
    b. classically conditioned emotional response
    c. irrational fear of pain
    d. vivid memory of the dog's attack

17. One difference between operant and classical conditioning is that in the former:
    a. responding produces no changes in the environment
    b. responding has an effect on the environment
    c. responding is more likely to be controlled by the CS
    d. responses do not generalize to other stimuli as easily

18. Thorndike found that the animals in his research:
    a. learned to escape confinement almost immediately after each session started
    b. had dificulty learning to escape at first, but then, in a flash of insight, learned to do so
    c. gradually took less and less time to escape as the experiment progressed
    d. only learned to escape confinement with great difficulty

19. When Jane was a little girl, she used to throw temper tantrums. At first, her parents showered lots of attention on her to get her to quiet down. Soon, though, her parents realized that her tantrums were becoming more frequent. As a result, they decided to completely ignore Jane's tantrums. Jane's tantrums first increased in both frequency and intensity. Gradually, though, they stopped altogether. Jane's parents had effectively employed what operant procedure in eliminating her tantrums?
   a. positive reinforcement
   b. punishment
   c. response cost
   d. extinction

20. The development of the bond between a mother and offspring is called:
   a. sexual imprinting
   b. fixed action pattern
   c. maternal imprinting
   d. adult imprinting

21. Intermittent reinforcement:
   a. eventually produces extinction
   b. involves reinforcing each response
   c. is a form of response cost
   d. involves non-reinforcement of some responses

22. If a response is reinforced, on average, after every 35 responses, what kind of reinforcement schedule is in effect?
   a. fixed-ratio
   b. variable-ratio
   c. variable-interval
   d. fixed-interval

23. If a response is reinforced, on average, after 60 seconds has elapsed since the previous reinforcer delivery, what kind of reinforcement schedule is in effect?
   a. fixed-interval
   b. fixed-ratio
   c. variable-ratio
   d. variable-interval

24. The hidden observer refers to:
   a. examining behavior in such a way that the experimental subject can not see you
   b. explanations of behavior in social situations
   c. explorations of social behavior in naturalistic settings
   d. a mental structure that monitors everything that happens

25. An example of _____ would be if you were to observe a rat pressing a lever in the presence of a 1000 Hz tone but not pressing the lever in the presence of a 700 Hz tone.
    a. discrimination
    b. generalization
    c. conditioned reinforcement
    d. intermittent reinforcement

26. Infantile amnesia or the loss of memories that occur early in life is probably due to:
    a. immature hippocampal development
    b. immature hypothalamic development
    c. motivated forgetting
    d. inadequate repetition
    e. none of the above

27. In a negative reinforcement procedure, an organism's responses:
    a. have no effect on the environment
    b. produce a punished response
    c. terminate or avoid an aversive stimulus
    d. produce a response cost

28. The rats in Garcia and Koelling's study avoided drinking water after they first experienced a pairing of:
    a. bright-noisy water and illness
    b. saccharine-flavored water and electric shock
    c. lemon-flavored water and illness
    d. saccharine-flavored water and illness

29. Learned helplessness refers to the fact that exposure to inescapable and uncontrollable aversive events produces passive behavior.
    a. True
    b. False

30. An animal who has been reinforced on a variable-interval schedule of reinforcement will respond:
    a. rapidly, receive the reinforcer, pause a little, and respond again
    b. more rapidly with each succeding reinforcement
    c. at a slow, steady rate
    d. faster then it would on a variable-ratio schedule

31. In classical conditioning, a learned response is said to be elicited by the unconditioned stimulus.
    a. True
    b. False

32. Rituals that accompany courtship in human cultures are acquired because of our inherited capacity for our behavior to be reinforced by environmental events.
    a. True
    b. False

33. One of the results from the famous Garcia and Koelling study (1966) was the finding that stimuli that arise internally (such as directing a stimuli's flavor) is more readily associated with an internal event (such as illness) than it is with an external event (such as electric shock applied to the skin).
    a. True
    b. False

34. One of the places in the brain that olfactory information is sent to is the _____ , which plays a role in both _____.
    a. limbic system; emotion and memory
    b. hypothalamus; homeostasis and thirst
    c. amydgala; emotion and aggression
    d. cerebellum; movement and coordination

35. The receptor cells for smell are located in the:
    a. nasal cavity
    b. olfactory mucosa
    c. olfactory bulb
    d. olfactory nerve

36. Recent research on olfaction in humans suggest that:
    a. there may be sex attractant pheromones such as those found in lower animals
    b. menstrual cycles in females are coordinated by their odors
    c. young infants can smell their own mother
    d. all of the above

37. Recent research indicates that the formation of new proteins may be involved in memory.
    a. True
    b. False

38. The "pleasure center" of the brain is located in the:
    a. central fissure
    b. cerebellum
    c. basal ganglia
    d. medial forebrain bundle

39. Memory in goldfish is disrupted by treatment with puromycin.
    a. True
    b. False

40. The type of memory that has the shortest duration is called _____ memory.
    a. sensory
    b. perceptual
    c. short-term
    d. episodic

41. Short-term memory:
    a. is also called working memory
    b. works on information that we have just perceived
    c. permits us to think about new information in terms of what we already know
    d. all of the above

42. The tendency to remember words at the beginning of a list is called the
    _____ effect.
    a. primacy
    b. recency
    c. encoding specificity
    d. consolidation

43. Suppose that you have been given a short list of words to memorize. After you have read through the list once, you discover that you remember the last four words on the list perfectly. This result is an example of the
    a. Peterson recall procedure
    b. proactive remembering
    c. primacy effect
    d. recency effect

44. Consolidation is the transference of information from _____ memory to _____ memory.
    a. long-term; short-term
    b. sensory; long-term
    c. sensory; short-term
    d. short-term; long-term

45. As she was driving to work, Alice was in a terrible auto accident. When she woke up in the hospital, she could not remember anything about the accident or what had happened to her just before that time. This is an example of what happens to people who have _____ amnesia.
    a. anterograde
    b. retrograde
    c. retroactive
    d. proactive

46. One important function of the hippocampus appears to be to influence the establishment of explicit long-term memories.
    a. True
    b. False

47. You could be said to be experiencing proactive interference in your ability to recall information if what you learned in a high school psychology class is interfering with your ability to recall information you are learning in your present psychology class.
    a. True
    b. False

48. Once the corpus callosum is severed, the two cerebral hemispheres:
    a. continue to exchange information
    b. regenerate most of the severed axons so they again can exchange information
    c. assume each other's functions
    d. function independently

49. When information is presented to the left visual field, a person with split-brain syndrome is unable to respond verbally to it because the:
    a. person is unable to perceive the information
    b. person does not perceive the information accurately
    c. information cannot be relayed to the language area of the brain
    d. information is lost in memory before the person can verbalize a description of it

50. We spend about _____ of our lives sleeping.
    a. one-sixth
    b. one-fifth
    c. one-fourth
    d. one-third

51. The apparatus that is used to measure the electrical activity of the brain is called an:
    a. electro-oculogram
    b. electromyogram
    c. electroencephalogram
    d. electrocardiogram

52. During periods of relaxation, EEG recordings of the brain's electrical activity generally show _____ activity.
    a. alpha
    b. beta
    c. theta
    d. delta

53. During slow wave or deep sleep, EEG recordings of the brain's electrical activity generally show_____ activity.
    a. alpha
    b. beta
    c. theta
    d. delta

54. REM involves all of the following characteristics except;
    a. rapid EEG waves
    b. dreams
    c. genital activity
    d. lack of muscular paralysis

55. Sleep deprivation has been found to interfere with:
    a. the ability to perform physical tasks
    b. the ability to react to stressful situations
    c. language abilities
    d. the ability to perform tasks that require vigilance

56. Lynn has been participating in a study investigating the effects of REM sleep deprivation. After several nights of being awakened just as she entered each period of REM sleep, she is allowed to sleep through the entire night. The polygraph revealed that on this night Lynn:
    a. slept about two hours longer than she normally does
    b. slept about two hours longer than she did when she was deprived of REM sleep
    c. spent the typical amount of time in REM sleep
    d. spent more time than normal in REM sleep

57. Research that has involved depriving non-human animals of REM sleep have found that REM sleep deprivation:
    a. does not affect normal development of the body
    b. may interfere with normal brain development
    c. is necessary for normal development of the limbic system
    d. affects animals' ability to navigate a radial arm maze

58. REM sleep-deprived subjects who are permitted to sleep normally again _____ during the next night or two.
    a. have difficulty entering REM sleep
    b. experience characteristics of REM sleep intruding in other sleep stages
    c. engage in many more bouts of REM sleep
    d. experience bouts of insomnia

59. The split brain operation involves severing the connections to either side of the central fissure.
    a. True
    b. False

60. Most people who frequently gamble are probably on a ____schedule of reinforcement.
    a. FR
    b. CRF
    c. VI
    d. VR
    e. None of the above

ANSWERS FOR PRACTICE EXAM #2

1. b	21. d	41. d
2. d	22. b	42. a
3. c	23. d	43. d
4. c	24. d	44. d
5. c	25. a	45. b
6. d	26. a	46. a
7. b	27. c	47. a
8. c	28. d	48. d
9. c	29. a	49. c
10. a	30. a	50. d
11. d	31. b	51. c
12. d	32. a	52. a
13. a	33. a	53. d
14. a	34. a	54. d
15. b	35. b	55. d
16. b	36. d	56. d
17. b	37. a	57. b
18. c	38. d	58. c
19. d	39. a	59. b
20. d	40. a	60. d

PRACTICE EXAM #3

1. The psychological experience of "hunger" is controlled by:
   a. blood/sugar levels
   b. glucoreceptors in the brain
   c. the VMN
   d. the LH
   e. all of the above

2. Schacter's experiments comparing obese people with normal people indicate that:
   a. obese people are plate cleaners
   b. obese people are more affected by the taste of food
   c. obese people are more likely to perform physical labor for food
   d. 'a' and 'b'
   e. none of the above

3. Hormones:
   a. are not essential for lower animal sexual behavior
   b. are necessary for human sexual behavior
   c. may influence the "arousability" of the human female
   d. are unnecessary for both human and lower animal sexual behavior
   e. none of the above

4. Hedonistic theories of motivation claim that people:
   a. seek novelty
   b. avoid pain
   c. pursue pleasure
   d. are instinctively aggressive
   e. 'b' and 'c'

5. Ward's research on prenatal stress effects shows that male rats exhibit:
   a. reduced feminine behavior and elevated masculine behavior.
   b. elevated feminine behavior and reduced masculine behavior.
   c. no changes in their sexual behavior.
   d. none of the above

6. A somewhat surprising finding from Stanley Schacter's laboratory was that overweight people are:
   a. willing to make great efforts and undergo pain to obtain food
   b. less willing to perform labor or undergo pain to obtain food
   c. less sensitive to the taste of food
   d. very sensitive to hunger signals from their bodies

7. Simon LeVay's research comparing the brains of homosexual and heterosexual men shows that :
   a. homosexual brains have less testosterone.
   b. heterosexual brains have less testosterone.
   c. their brains are different in several hypothalamic nuclei.
   d. all of the above

8. A woman undergoes an operation to have both ovaries removed. Will she still be interested in and able to engage in the same sexual activities?
   a. yes, ovaries produce eggs, not hormones
   b. yes, her sexuality is determined by much more than hormonal levels
   c. yes, androgens will take over for the reduced estrogen levels
   d. no, her interest and ability regarding sex will diminish over time

9. Binet was interested in distinguishing between:
   a. specially talented children from children without special talents
   b. children of different brain size
   c. smart children from children who would have problems in school
   d. average from brilliant children

10. If you took the same IQ test once a month for six months and got the same score each time, you would conclude the test was:
    a. valid
    b. reliable
    c. fair
    d. scored in percentiles

11. In Terman's long term study of gifted children, he found that success in adult life was strongly associated with:
    a. rich parents
    b. a warm and stimulating home environment that emphasized the importance of education
    c. personality factors such as self confidence, goal oriented behavior, and perseverance
    d. sibling role models
    e. all of the above

12. Dave is castrated in adulthood because of cancer. This would tend to block
_____ effects of testosterone.
   a. only organizational
   b. only activational
   c. both organizational and activational
   d. neither organizational nor activational

13. Debbie is experiencing a higher-than-usual level of sexual arousal. All else held
equal, you might expect that she was at the_____ of her menstrual cycle.
   a. beginning
   b. middle
   c. end
   d. either b or c

14. The testosterone levels of homosexual males are _____those of heterosexual
males:
   a. less than
   b. greater than
   c. the same as
   d. none of the above

15. Field studies of long-term viewing of violence on television suggest that
_____ :
   a. children who watch television violence should engage in physical activities to
      channel their feelings
   b. the more closely violent television situations resemble the child's
      environment, the greater the effect will be
   c. young children are more vulnerable than older children to the effects of
      television violence
   d. long-term viewing appears to increase aggressive behavior, but the evidence
      is not definitive

16. Studies of black and interracial children adopted into white families show that
the IQs of the adopted children are _____ the national average.
   a. lower than
   b. the same as
   c. higher than
   d. none of the above

17. Skeel's study demonstrated that placing neglected institutionalized children who have low IQ scores with retarded foster mothers generally led to _____ in the children's IQs.
    a. no consistent effect
    b. no change
    c. a decrease
    d. an increase

18. A 20-year old with a mental age of the average 12 year old would have an IQ _____ .
    a. of 83
    b. equal to the average IQ of a 12 year old child
    c. equal to 1.3 times the average IQ of the 12 year old child
    d. of 60

19. Identical twins reared apart tend to:
    a. have dissimilar IQs
    b. have IQs that are more similar than fraternal twins reared together
    c. have IQs that are less similar than fraternal twins reared apart
    d. none of the above

20. Prenatal progesterone exposure in human females_____:
    a. reduces cognitive abilities
    b. feminizes the brain
    c. promotes aggressive attitudes and behaviors
    d. elevates spatial abilities

21. Skeel's research is important because he showed that:
    a. a stimulating environment can raise intellectual functioning
    b. intelligence is crystallized at puberty
    c. intelligence is set at birth and is not easily influenced
    d. love and affection can raise IQ

22. Arthur Jensen attributes observed differences in the IQs of blacks and whites to:
    a. environmental influences
    b. genetic influences
    c. cultural bias
    d. unreliable tests

23. The famous case of the identical twins John and Joan suggests that:
    a. hormones play no role in psychosexual identity
    b. hormones can't be responsible for differences in aggressive behavior
    c. hormone exposure early in life may be responsible for establishing psychosexual identity
    d. none of the above

24. Concordance research with identical twins suggest that:
    a. there may be a genetic cause for lesbianism
    b. the link between genes and sexual orientation may be remote
    c. there may be a genetic cause for homosexuality
    d. a and c

25. Which of the following statements regarding the effects of child care are true?
    a. Children who are in day care tend to be low achievers in school.
    b. The quality of child care is a key factor in promoting secure attachment in early childhood and preventing problems in later childhood.
    c. Low quality day care can potentially contribute to social and academic problems in later childhood.
    d. High quality day are centers, where they exist, tend to be expensive and may have long waiting lists.
    e. b, c, and d

26. In the Harlow's research, the only "monster" mother that the infant monkey rejected was the one which:
    a. contained a catapult
    b. contained metal spikes
    c. contained ice water in its veins
    d. blasted the infant with compressed air

27. According to Harlow's research, the infant's "love" of the mother is primarily a response to the _____ of the mother during the first two weeks of life, and after this _____ becomes paramount.
    a. contact comfort; food
    b. warmth; contact comfort
    c. eyes; the smell of the mother
    d. warmth; food

28. In the small Canadian town called NOTEL, psychologists found_____
after television programming became available.
   a. increased rates of narcolepsy
   b. reduced rates of sleep disorders
   c. elevated rates of petty crimes
   d. increased incidence of eating disorders
   e. none of the above

29. Washoe:
   a. learned a sign language called American Sign Language
   b. was able to string three and four words together in short sentences
   c. showed some overextensions in her language use
   d. all of the above

30. Imitative behavior in newborns is:
   a. virtually absent until about 2 to 3 months of age
   b. limited because of the newborn's immature visual capacities and lack of coordination
   c. simply a reflex
   d. unsubstantiated by most scientific studies
   e. none of the above

31. Research such as Project Washoe is useful because it:
   a. confirms Darwin's theory of language acquisition
   b. demonstrates the uniqueness of human language abilities
   c. confirms the existence of the language acquisition device
   d. investigates the evolutionary continuity of the ability to communicate

32. The first intelligence measure developed by Binet and Simon (1905) was intended to:
   a. establish intellectual norms for the French population
   b. identify children who could benefit from special academic instruction
   c. measure the intelligence of preschoolers
   d. identify gifted children

33. An important criticism of intelligence testing is that intelligence tests:
   a. measure achievement
   b. may be culturally biased
   c. can be used unfairly to deny people access to certain opportunities
   d. all of the above

34. Men are more likely to fantasize dominance themes (forcing someone to do something sexual) while women are more likely to report submission themes (being forced to do something sexual).
    a. True
    b. False

35. Peter and Paul are identical twins who were given up for adoptions shortly after they were born. Peter was raised by well-educated parents, but Paul was not. It is likely that Peter and Paul have:
    a. identical IQ scores because they are identical twins
    b. very different IQ scores because they were raised in very different environments
    c. similar IQ scores because they are identical twins
    d. none of the above

36. The assertions made in the book *The Bell Curve* are weakened by the fact that:
    a. not all psychologists agree that intelligence is due to a single factor
    b. there is not a consensus as to what intelligence really is
    c. IQ is, in fact, modifiable to a certain extent
    d. all of the above

37. A person's genetic endowment places limits on the extent to which the brain develops and intelligence may develop.
    a. True
    b. False

38. In the absence of _____ the fetus becomes a female.
    a. teratogens
    b. androgens
    c. estrogens
    d. norepinephrine

39. If an object is completely hidden from view after a 12-16 month old infant has observed it, the infant will:
    a. lose interest in the object
    b. continue to stare at the spot at which the object disappeared
    c. begin crying and screaming
    d. search for the object in the last place that he or she saw it hidden

40. Children who are in the early phases of the preoperational stage cannot master which of the following?
    a. object permanence
    b. conservation
    c. deferred imitation
    d. very simple symbolic reasoning

41. Mary pours the same amount of apple juice into two glasses. However, one of the glasses is taller and skinnier than the other. Pete and Mike both want the taller glass because they think it contains more juice. Apparently neither Pete nor Mike:
    a. can reason symbolically
    b. understands the concept of object permanence
    c. is developing an ability for deferred imitation
    d. has yet mastered the principle of conservation

42. Although Piaget's theory has proven to be a useful one, it has been criticized on the grounds that:
    a. not all formal operational adolescents can reason abstractly
    b. it overlooks Case and Fisher's work on information processing in children
    c. it underestimates the intellectual sophistication of children and adolescents
    d. concrete operational children can actually master object permanence

43. Non-human animal research suggests that early exposure to _____ can produce long-term effects on behavior. These effects have important implications for understanding _____ .
    a. male hormones; gender differences in behavior
    b. particular transmitter substances; gender role differences
    c. female hormones; childrearing practices
    d. particular neuromodulators; sexual orientation

44. Television viewing by children detracts from their reading achievement.
    a. True
    b. False

45. Which of the following drives is not based on homeostasis?
    a. hunger
    b. sex
    c. thirst
    d. warmth

46. The glucostatic hypothesis asserts that hunger occurs when the amount of
_____ in the blood is _____.
    a. glycogen; high
    b. flycogen; low
    c. glucose; high
    d. glucose; low

47. Penny is a 19 year old college student who is obsessed with her body weight.
She feels that she is too heavy, even though she weighs only 100 pounds (she
is 5' 1" tall). She will sometimes go for several days without eating food but will
drink large amounts of diet soda. Occasionally she will go on an eating
rampage, consuming large quantities of food, only to relieve herself using
laxatives. What would you diagnose Penny's eating problem to be?
    a. obesity
    b. anorexia nervosa
    c. bulimia
    d. both anorexia and bulimia

48. Women who take oral contraceptives:
    a. enjoy sexual intercourse more than women who use other forms of birth
       control
    b. show little fluctuation in sexual interest across the menstrual cycle
    c. show peaks of sexual activity during the third week of the menstrual cycle
    d. show decreased sexual desire compared to women who use other forms of
       birth control

49. The single most important predictor of homosexuality is:
    a. gender nonconformity
    b. having an overprotective mother and an indifferent father
    c. the report of homosexual feelings long before the first homosexual
       experience
    d. high levels of testosterone

50. Mark the mouse was raised in a cage all by himself. When he was about 6
months old, Mickey the mouse was placed into Mark's cage. However, Mark did
not attack Mickey. Mark's lack of aggression suggests that:
    a. Mickey was castrated early in life
    b. Mickey immediately made an appeasement gesture
    c. Mark immediately made an appeasement gesture
    d. Mark was castrated early in life

51. The rationale for giving antiandrogens to sex offenders is that it is:
    a. more effective than castration
    b. based on non-human animal research that androgens can cause sexual and aggressive behaviors
    c. more effective than traditional forms of psychotherapy
    d. none of the above

52. The head-dipping response of the three-spined stickleback fish is a classic example of:
    a. marital problems
    b. a fixed action pattern
    c. displacement behavior
    d. the frustration-aggression hypothesis

53. Darwin argued that emotional expressions in people and in non-human animals are:
    a. learned
    b. innate
    c. composed of simple movements of face, neck and head
    d. primarily reactions to aversive environmental events

54. If you were to find yourself in some remote area of the world inhabited by people who, heretofore, were unknown to the rest of the world, you would:
    a. not be able to recognize any of their facial expressions of emotion.
    b. be able to recognize only their facial expressions of anger and happiness.
    c. have great difficulty recognizing any of their facial expressions of emotion.
    d. be able to recognize many of their facial expressions of emotion.

55. Jill has just struck out with the bases loaded in the bottom of the final inning of an important softball game. Her team lost by only one run. In the dugout, she attempts to hold back her anger by gently putting her batting helmet and bat into the gear bag. Her attempt to minimize her emotional expression is an example of:
    a. modulation
    b. simulation
    c. deception
    d. none of the above

56. The idea that the experience of emotion is preceded by physiological arousal is called the _____ theory of emotion.
    a. Cannon-Bard
    b. two-factor
    c. James-Lange
    d. Schacter-Singer

57. Anthony is a paraplegic and Lenore is a quadriplegic. If queried about the intensity of their emotions:
   a. Anthony would most likely report more intense feelings
   b. Lenore would most likely report more intense feelings
   c. They both would report having about the same level of feelings
   d. Lenore would report having little or no feelings about anything

58. Drives:
   a. have behavioral effects opposite to those of reinforcement
   b. are only produced by homeostatic imbalances
   c. cannot be directly measured
   d. are involved in reinforcement, but not in punishment

59. Field studies of long-term viewing of violence on television suggest that:
   a. it would be prudent to have children who watch television violence engage in vigorous physical activity to discharge their feelings
   b. the more closely violent television situations resemble the child's actual environment the greater their effect will be
   c. young children are more vulnerable than older children to the effects of television violence
   d. long-term viewing appears to increase aggressive behavior, but the evidence is not conclusive

60. During a single meal, eating will stop after eating a relatively nutritious food, but will continue for a longer time if the food is not very nutritious.
   a. True
   b. False

ANSWERS FOR PRACTICE EXAM #3

1. e	21. a	41. d
2. d	22. b	42. c
3. c	23. c	43. a
4. e	24. d	44. b
5. b	25. e	45. b
6. b	26. c	46. d
7. c	27. b	47. d
8. b	28. e	48. b
9. c	29. d	49. c
10. b	30. e	50. d
11. c	31. d	51. b
12. b	32. b	52. b
13. b	33. d	53. b
14. c	34. a	54. d
15. d	35. c	55. a
16. c	36. d	56. c
17. d	37. a	57. a
18. d	38. b	58. c
19. b	39. d	59. d
20. c	40. b	60. a

PRACTICE EXAM #4

1. The items used in the MMPI test of personality were selected on the basis of:
    a. the responses of mental patients and normal persons to the items
    b. Freud's theory of personality
    c. Allport's theory of personality
    d. Psychiatric judgment

2. The _____ test is an example of a projective test.
    a. Stanford-Binet
    b. Binet-Simon
    c. TAT
    d. MMPI

3. Electro-convulsive shock therapy is most likely to be used for those persons who are:
    a. severely depressed
    b. anti-social
    c. extremely aggressive
    d. hyper-emotional

4. Max Jones believed that:
    a. mental illness is like physical illness
    b. patients can play an active role in their treatment
    c. psychotherapy could relieve almost all mental disorders
    d. most mental patients are irresponsible with respect their own treatment

5. Mental health care in the United States today is characterized by:
    a. community mental health centers
    b. custodial care
    c. therapeutic communities
    d. exorcism

6. Transforming the expression of a repressed motive to its opposite is called:
    a. fixation
    b. archetype
    c. superego
    d. reaction formation

7. According to Abraham Maslow, meta needs are:
    a. represented in metaphysical values
    b. spiritual values
    c. essential for complete human development
    d. essential to prevent alienation

e. all of the above

8. The primary drawback(s) to the statistical criterion of normality is (are):
   a. it is specific to time and place
   b. it doesn't distinguish between desirable and undesirable behavior
   c. statistics are unreliable
   d. all of the above
   e. 'a' and 'b'

9. According to Thomas Szasz, mental disorders are:
   a. primarily biological
   b. curable only by extensive use of drugs and electroconvulsive therapy
   c. not curable
   d. problems in living which in the final analysis are solvable only by the person who has them

10. Freud and Jung strongly disagree about the functions of the:
    a. libido
    b. ego
    c. reservoir of fears
    d. conscious

11. Animus is to anima as:
    a. masculine is to feminine
    b. archetype is to collective unconscious
    c. collective unconscious is to personal unconscious
    d. feminine is to masculine

12. Clinical neuroses is characterized by:
    a. depression
    b. mood swings
    c. bodily symptoms like headaches
    d. all of the above

13. The principle goal of halfway house programs is:
    a. to reduce levels of schizophrenia
    b. provide therapy without separating a person from their community
    c. reduce the number of large mental hospitals and shift care over to local clinics
    d. b and c

14. You describe your psychology professor as warm, intelligent, competent and creative. Allport would label these:
    a. cardinal traits
    b. central traits
    c. secondary traits
    d. learned traits

15. All of the various social-behavioral therapies are based on the assumption that mental disorders are caused by:
    a. a person's inner psychodynamics
    b. disturbed relationships between people
    c. early childhood traumas
    d. biochemical factors

16. Jack received 5 points for eating a nutritional breakfast, 10 points for attending and participating in an interaction group, and 5 points for cleaning up the TV lounge. The mental hospital he is in is using:
    a. a token economy
    b. client-centered therapy
    c. jump start therapy
    d. gestalt therapy

17. The results of Milgram's compliance studies show that a significant percentage of people will _____ .
    a. follow orders of authority figures as long as no harmful effects results for others
    b. not follow orders of authority figures when they disagree with the order
    c. follow orders of authority figures even when harmful effects on others are the result
    d. stop following orders of authority figures when the situation results in physical harm, but no psychological harm for others

18. Bandura's experiments with the "bobo" dolls have shows that children learn by _____ .
    a. positive reinforcement
    b. negative reinforcement
    c. watching others
    d. punishment

19. In which defense mechanism are unacceptable drives diverted into acceptable activities?
    a. sublimation
    b. projection
    c. rationalization
    d. reaction formation

20. Many baseball players go through a ritual every time they step to the plate. For example, they might tap their bat on the plate 3 times, or twitch their arm, or adjust their batting helmet with the end of the bat. These behaviors are probably a form of _____ .
    a. obsession
    b. phobia
    c. delusion
    d. compulsion

21. The most frequently used antipsychotic drugs are:
    a. reserpine and valium
    b. reserpine and prozac
    c. prozac and lithium
    d. lithium and Imipramine
    e. lithium and chlorpromazine

22. The following is (are) true regarding antipsychotic drugs:
    a. they affect substance P
    b. they are effective in reducing hallucinations
    c. they influence the dopamine system
    d. a and b
    e. b and c

23. Pillippe Pinel is most famous for his _____ .
    a. invention of frontal lobotomies
    b. belief that most mental patients would respond to treatment
    c. contributions to insight psychotherapy
    d. development of structural family therapy

24. The following is (are) true regarding the use of drugs to treat behavior disorders:
    a. there are significant side effects, like tardive dyskenesis, that can result from prolonged drug treatment
    b. non drug treatments, like herbs for example, can work just as well
    c. drugs often only remove symptoms but not underlying causes of disorders
    d. all of the above

25. Ted acts out the role of one of his group members, while that group member pretends to be someone else. What type of group therapy might Paul be involved in?
    a. family therapy
    b. psychodrama
    c. insight
    d. antianxiety therapy

26. St. John's Wort is an herb hat is most effective in the treatment of :
    a. schizophrenia
    b. manic depression
    c. genital warts
    d. affective disorders
    e. none of the above

27. Studies on the effectiveness of psychotherapy indicate that the therapy is

    _____ .
    a. at best not harmful
    b. consistently beneficial
    c. more or less effective depending upon the client's mental health at the time treatment begins
    d. all of the above

28. The rationale for giving antiandrogens to sex offenders is
    a. it is useless to castrate an offender.
    b. the efficiency of the treatment has been established.
    c. animal research indicates androgens promote sexual and aggressive behavior.
    d. males are more aggressive and sexual than females.

29. Ann persistently complains of a number of physical pains. These have included headaches, chronic stomach aches and a sharpness of pain in her chest area. Over the years, Ann has had a number of medical tests but her doctors have been unable to find anything physically wrong with her. Ann is suffering from:
    a. conversion disorder.
    b. hypochondriasis.
    c. dissociative disorder.
    d. somatization disorder.

30. Projective personality tests:
    a. measure the degree to which a subject agrees or disagrees with the examiner's interpretation of an ambiguous situation.
    b. are based on the assumption that an ambiguous situation will elicit the subject's true feelings.
    c. are not as difficult to score as empirical tests.
    d. require that subject responses be realistic.

31. It is difficult to evaluate psychoanalysis because:
    a. most informants were dissatisfied with treatment and do not constitute a random sample.
    b. failure is often attributed to the client and not to the treatment.
    c. the goals of therapy are not defined in ways that can be measured.
    d. behavioral change is more important than understanding the cause of the behavior.

32. Behavior therapies are based on the assumption that:
    a. symptom substitution is an important problem with insight therapy.
    b. people are basically good and problems are the result of faulty learning.
    c. a sound scientific basis reduces the importance of the therapist.
    d. behavioral change is more important than understanding the cause of the behavior.

33. The most important objection to the use of electroconvulsive therapy is:
    a. even a few treatments produce brain damage and excessive use results in permanent memory loss.
    b. it is generally too slow-acting to be effective treatment for depression.
    c. it is very difficult to evaluate the therapeutic effects of a treatment that produces permanent brain damage.
    d. even a few treatments blunt the effect of antidepressant drugs.

34. Subjects who were asked to estimate the length of lines went along with the group decision in spite of some doubts. This suggests that:
    a. group pressure affects perceptions as well as behavior.
    b. the subjects found other members of the group to be attractive.
    c. the pressure to conform can be very strong.
    d. group pressure increases self-esteem.

35. The majority of subjects in a series of experiment on obedience by Milgram:
    a. urged other subjects to shock the learner too.
    b. repeatedly shocked the learner in spite of obvious signs of his distress.
    c. asked the experimenter to confirm that the learner would not suffer permanent harm.
    d. stopped shocking the learner at the first signs of his distress.

36. People tend to choose:
    a. partners who are about as physically attractive as they are.
    b. the most attractive partner they can.
    c. a less attractive partner to reduce the likelihood of rejection.
    d. a less attractive partner because they tend to have more interesting personalities.

37. The most prevalent disorder in the US is _____ .
    a. antisocial personality disorder.
    b. mood disturbance.
    c. substance abuse disorder.
    d. schizophrenia.

38. An irresistible urge to repeat an action over and over again is called a(n):
    a. obsession.
    b. compulsion.
    c. phobia.
    d. fetish.

39. Ted Bundy is an example of a person who suffered from:
    a. paranoid schizophrenia.
    b. psychogenic fugue.
    c. antisocial personality disorder.
    d. conversion disorder.

40. Pete is convinced that he is the son of god and the savior of the world. Pete appears to be experiencing delusions of:
    a. grandeur.
    b. control.
    c. persecution.
    d. power.

41. Suppose that you are a clinical psychologist and are treating a person who shows the following symptoms: flattened emotional responses, poverty of speech, social withdrawal, and inability to experience pleasure. Your best course of action in treating the person's symptoms is to use:
    a. electroconvulsive shock therapy.
    b. psychotherapy.
    c. psychosurgery.
    d. radiation therapy.

42. The antidepressant drugs appear to have stimulating effects on synapses that involve the transmitter substances _____ and _____.
    a. epinephrine; serotonin
    b. acetylcholine; dopamine
    c. norepinephrine; serotonin
    d. reserpine; GABA

43. _____ is a mood disorder characterized by lethargy, sleep disturbances, and a craving for carbohydrates.
    a. Bipolar disorder
    b. Major depression
    c. Seasonal affective disorder
    d. Dythymic disorder

44. The Diagnostic and Statistical Manual of APA:
    a. discourages treatment of hopeless cases.
    b. facilitates research on the causes and treatments of mental disorders.
    c. is cross-indexed to accepted treatments.
    d. eliminates the possibility of multiple diagnoses.

45. When we say that schizophrenia is a heritable disease, we mean that:
    a. a person who has inherited a "schizophrenia gene" will eventually develop the disease.
    b. A person inherits a tendency toward schizophrenia which may be triggered in certain environments.
    c. The liklihood of a person with a "schizophrenia gene" developing the disease is influenced solely by the biological family history.
    d. It is not possible to carry an unexpressed "schizophrenia gene."

46. Psychologist Diana Baumrind attacked Milgram's Obedience studies because she felt that:
    a. Milgram's studies caused the subjects emotional stress, tension, and loss of dignity
    b. Milgram's studies did not use sound experimental methods
    c. Milgram had copied Baumrind's earlier work
    d. The subject's in Milgram's study were not adequately debriefed
    e. all of the above

47. The earliest know attempt to treat mental disorders involved:
    a. trephining.
    b. implosive therapy.
    c. sorcery.
    d. prefrontal lobotomies.
48. Which of the following are true regarding the insanity pleas as a legal defense?

a. The verdict called "guilty but mentally ill" is rarely used in US courts.
b. Actual cases of acquittal by reason of insanity are frequent.
c. A defendant may be found not guilty by reason of insanity only if he were so severely disturbed at the time of his act that he did not know that it was wrong.
d. Accused people who are mentally ill frequently come to trial.
e. All of the above.

49. Rick has been undergoing therapy for the past several months. During the therapy sessions, his therapist has asked him to "just sort of talk about anything that comes to mind." She has also asked him about his dreams. Most likely, Rudy's therapist is a _____ therapist.
a. psychoanalyst or psychodynamic
b. client-centered
c. rational-emotive
d. cognitive-behavioral

50. The tendency of clients in psychoanalysis to project their attitudes and emotions onto the therapist as a result of "reliving" some of their unpleasant childhood experiences is called:
a. projection.
b. transference.
c. displacement.
d. sublimation

51. Therapy that helps the client close the gap between his or her real self and ideal self is called:
a. gestalt-therapy
b. client-centered therapy.
c. rational-emotive therapy.
d. cognitive-behavior therapy.

52. Dan is petrified of snakes. To help him overcome his fear, his therapist is teaching Dan to relax in the face of increasingly more realistic encounters with a snake. First, Dan simply imagines the snake, then he imagines that a snake placed in a box is brought into the room, and so on, until he finally imagines himself holding the reptile. He implements the relaxation procedures his therapist has taught him each time he imagines a different "snake scenario." Dan's therapist is using the therapeutic technique called:
a. rational-emotive therapy.
b. aversion therapy.
c. modeling.
d. systematic desensitization.

53. Who among the following would be considered the family therapist's "client" if an entire family is present for therapy?
a. the head of the household
b. the entire family as a unit
c. the individual in the family who has the most serious personal problems
d. each individual member of the family

54. A community treatment program that functions primarily to help make the transition from living in a mental institution to living in a regular community is the:
a. community mission.
b. group home.
c. halfway house.
d. community mental health center.

55. Prozac, the newest behavioral wonder drug, has made many health professionals uncomfortable since it is being overprescribed and often prescribed for the wrong reasons.
a. True
b. False

56. Eysenck's early study of the effectiveness of psychotherapy showed that:
a. humanistic therapy was more effective than cognitive-behavior therapy
b. psychoanalysis was the least effective of the therapies that he studied.
c. rational-emotive therapy was the most effective of the cognitive-behavior therapies.
d. none of the different therapies were especially effective.

57. A long-term, negative side effect of using antipsychotic drugs to treat schizophrenia is a serious movement disorder called:
a. cystic fibrosis
b. tardive dyskinesia.
c. cerebellar impairment.
d. none of the above.

58. ECT is most often used to treat:
a. schizophrenia.
b. severe depression.
c. dissociative disorders.
d. generalized anxiety disorders.

59. The court ruling in the Tarasoff case and others has made it clear that when a therapist is working with a potentially violent client, the therapist:
    a. has the responsibility to inform law authorities about the individual.
    b. has the responsibility to warn potential victims.
    c. may be held liable for the client's violent behavior.
    d. all of the above.

60. The ongoing "Minnesota Study of Twins Reared Apart" has show:
    a. very few similarities in the occupations, hobbies, personality traits, and habits of identical twins that were separated at birth
    b. that similarities in identical twins reared apart are probably due to coincidence
    c. that there are many profound differences as well as similarities between identical twins reared apart
    d. none of the above

ANSWERS FOR PRACTICE EXAM #4

1. a	21. e	41. b
2. c	22. e	42 c
3. a	23. b	43. c
4. b	24. d	44. b
5. a	25. b	45. b
6. d	26. e	46. a
7. e	27. d	47. a
8. e	28. c	48. c
9. d	29. d	49. a
10. a	30. b	50. b
11. a	31. c	51. b
12. d	32. d	52. d
13. d	33. a	53. b
14. b	34. c	54. c
15. b	35. b	55. a
16. a	36. a	56. d
17. c	37. c	57. b
18. c	38. b	58. b
19. a	39. c	59. d
20. d	40. a	60. c

PRACTICE QUIZ #1

Answer True or False

1. The founder of modern experimental psychotherapy was Sir Francis Galton.

2. In a typical psychology experiment, the experimental group is exposed to the treatment.

3. In the double blind technique, neither the experimenter nor the subject know who is in the experimental group and who is in the control group.

4. Charles Darwin was one of the first scientists to examine the effects of artificial selection on behavior.

5. Our phenotype is a product of genes and the environment.

6. The new brain consists of the limbic system and basal ganglia.

7. Serotonin may be responsible for cuddling in humans.

8. Edward Thorndike was the father of classical conditioning.

9. In classical conditioning, the CS must precede the UCS for conditioning to take place.

10. Pavlov showed that the passage of time could serve as a conditioned stimulus.

11. The learning curve discovered by Thorndike shows that performance gets better with reinforced practice.

12. CRF means core reinforcement factor.

13. Neal Miller showed that autonomic responses could be operantly conditioned.

14. In Watson's famous experiment with Little Albert, the CS was the loud noise.

15. The visual cliff apparatus measures extra sensory perception.

16. Perception research shows that scrambled faces are preferred over normal faces.

17. The serial position curve shows that our memory is not very good following short-term transfer.

18. REM deprivation can improve both long term and short term memory.

19. The EEG machine measures electrical activity of the brain.

20. Extinction of an operant response occurs when we no longer deliver reinforcement.

PRACTICE QUIZ #2

Answer True or False

1.. Piaget's Theory states that there must be a balance between assimilation and accommodation.

2. Negative reinforcement is the same thing as punishment.

3. The MMPI is an example of a projective test.

4. Our sensory store has an unlimited storage capacity.

5. Harlow found that the only monster mother that produced long lasting rejection was the spike mother.

6. Ted Bundy created the first standard intelligence test.

7. The concordance rate for IQs is much higher in fraternal twins than identical twins.

8. Gary Lynch showed improved memory in goldfish following puromycin injections.

9. The vomeronasal organ might be responsible for aggressive behavior in children.

10. Lesions of the lateral hypothalamus tend to produce aphagia and adipsia.

11. REM sleep is characterized by high amplitude, low frequency waves.

12. Stanley Migram's research shows that disobedience to the commands of an authority figure is likely to occur when there is no face to face contact with the authority.

13. During REM sleep, we usually show ALPHA brain wave patterns.

14. St. Johns Wort can be used to successfully treat mild depression.

15. Tardive dyskinesis occurs when mentally retarded patients lose depth perception.

16. Rats with ventromedial hypothalamic lesions won't tolerate mild shock to obtain food.

17. Instincts are objects or conditions in the environment that stimulate behavior.

18. Cocaine is a positive reinforcer.

19. The sentence completion test is an example of a projective test.

20. The statistical criterion states that normality is a goal we are all striving for in life.

PRACTICE QUIZ ANSWERS

Quiz #1	Quiz #2
1. False	1. True
2. True	2. False
3. True	3. False
4. True	4. False
5. True	5. False
6. False	6. False
7. False	7. False
8. False	8. False
9. True	9. False
10. True	10. True
11. True	11. False
12. False	12. True
13. True	13. True
14. False	14. True
15. False	15. False
16. False	16. True
17. False	17. False
18. False	18. True
19. True	19. True
20. True	20. False